Learn Portuguese In 7 DAYS!

The Ultimate Crash Course to Learning the Basics of the Portuguese Language in No Time

By Dagny Taggart
& Olívia Junqueira

© **Copyright 2015**

All rights reserved. No portion of this book may be reproduced -mechanically, electronically, or by any other means, including photocopying- without the permission of the publisher.

Disclaimer

The information provided in this book is designed to provide helpful information on the subjects discussed. The author's books are only meant to provide the reader with the basics knowledge of a certain language, without any warranties regarding whether the student will, or will not, be able to incorporate and apply all the information provided. Although the writer will make her best effort share her insights, language learning is a difficult task, and each person needs a different timeframe to fully incorporate a new language. This book, nor any of the author's books constitute a promise that the reader will learn a certain language within a certain timeframe.

Table of Contents

MY FREE GIFT TO YOU! 6

>> GET THE FULL PORTUGUESE ONLINE COURSE WITH AUDIO LESSONS << 7

SECTION 1: THE BASICS 12

    CHAPTER 1: Getting the Pronunciation Down 13
    CHAPTER 2: Portuguese and English differences and Basic Grammar 20
    CHAPTER 3: Greetings, Introductions, and Other Useful Phrases 26
    CHAPTER 4: About Time - Telling time, Days of Week, Dates 33
    CHAPTER 5: How Do You Like This Weather? 38

SECTION 2: IN THE CITY AND TRAVELLING 41

    CHAPTER 6: Directions 42
    CHAPTER 7: Shopping 47
    CHAPTER 8: Going out to eat 53
    CHAPTER 9: Going to the Doctor 59
    CHAPTER 10: Going to the Bank 66
    CHAPTER 11: Transportation 69
    CHAPTER 12: Finding a place to stay 78

SECTION 3: GETTING TO KNOW EACH OTHER 81

    CHAPTER 13: Description 82
    CHAPTER 14: We are family 88
    CHAPTER 15: All work and no play 92
    CHAPTER 16: Hobbies 96

SECTION 4: GRAMMAR SCHOOL 99

    CHAPTER 17: To be or not to be 100
    CHAPTER 18: Por e para 105
    CHAPTER 19: Conjugating Regular Verbs in the Present 108
    CHAPTER 20: Ter ou não Ter 116
    CHAPTER 21: Portuguese Around the World 120

    CONCLUSION: Now, Embark on Your Own Adventure! 125

>> GET THE FULL PORTUGUESE ONLINE COURSE WITH AUDIO LESSONS << ...126

PS: CAN I ASK YOU A QUICK FAVOR? 127

PREVIEW OF "LEARN SPANISH IN 7 DAYS! - THE ULTIMATE CRASH COURSE TO LEARN THE BASICS OF THE SPANISH LANGUAGE IN NO TIME" 128

CHECK OUT MY OTHER BOOKS 135

ABOUT THE AUTHOR..136

*Dedicated to those who love going beyond their own frontiers.
Keep on traveling,*

Dagny Taggart

My FREE Gift to You!

As a way of saying thank you for downloading my book, I'd like to send you an exclusive gift that will revolutionize the way you learn new languages. It's an extremely comprehensive PDF with 15 language hacking rules that **will help you learn 300% faster, with less effort, and with higher than ever retention rates**.

This guide is an amazing complement to the book you just got, and could easily be a stand-alone product, but for now I've decided to give it away for free, to thank you for being such an awesome reader, and to make sure I give you all the value that I can to help you succeed faster on your language learning journey.

To get your FREE gift, go to the link below, write down your email address and I'll send it right away!

>> http://bitly.com/PortugueseGift <<

>> Get The Full Portuguese Online Course With Audio Lessons <<

If you truly want to learn Portuguese 300% FASTER, then hear this out.

I've partnered with the most revolutionary language teachers to bring you the very best Portuguese online course I've ever seen. It's a mind-blowing program specifically created for language hackers such as ourselves. It will allow you learn Portuguese 3x faster, straight from the comfort of your own home, office, or wherever you may be. It's like having an unfair advantage!

The Online Course consists of:

+ 185 Built-In Lessons
+ 98 Interactive Audio Lessons
+ 24/7 Support to Keep You Going

The program is extremely engaging, fun, and easy-going. You won't even notice you are learning a complex foreign language from scratch. And before you realize it, by the time you go through all the lessons you will officially become a truly solid Portuguese speaker.

Old classrooms are a thing of the past. It's time for a language revolution.

If you'd like to go the extra mile, follow the link below and let the revolution begin

>> http://www.bitly.com/Portuguese-Course <<

CHECK OUT THE COURSE »

Introduction

Seja bem vindo!

Brazil is an amazing country, though you won't hear that from Brazilians a lot. Unfortunately, differently from other countries in South America, Europe and even Asia most people there don't speak any languages other than Portuguese, which makes traveling there a bit tricky for foreigners native to any languages other than theirs.

Most people are daunted by the idea of learning a language. They think it's impossible, even unfathomable. I remember as a junior in high school, watching footage of Jackie O giving a speech in French. I was so impressed and inspired by the ease at which she spoke this other language of which I could not understand one single word.

At that moment, I knew I had to learn at least one foreign language. I started with Portuguese, later took on Mandarin, and most recently have started learning Spanish. No matter how challenging and unattainable it may seem, millions of people have done it. You do NOT have to be a genius to learn another language. You DO have to be willing to take risks and make mistakes, sometimes even make a fool of yourself, be dedicated, and of course, practice, practice, practice!

This book will only provide you with the basics in order to get started learning Brazilian Portuguese. It is geared towards those who are planning to travel to Brazil and covers many common scenarios you may find yourself in so feel free to skip around to the topic that is most prudent to you at the moment. Even tough it is focused on Brazilian Portuguese you will find the key differences and similarities it shares with European Portuguese in Chapter 21. Keep in mind, every Portuguese-speaking country has some language details specific to them so it would be essential to do some research on the specific country or countries that you will visit.

I will now list some tips that I have found useful and should be very helpful to you in your journey of learning Portuguese. I don't wish you luck because that will not get you anywhere- reading this book, dedicating yourself, and taking some risks will!

Language Tips

Tip #1 - Keep an Open Mind

It may seem obvious but you must understand that languages are very different from each other. You cannot expect them to translate word for word. *'There is a black dog'* will not translate word for word with the same word order in Portuguese. You have to get used to the idea of translating WHOLE ideas. So don't find yourself saying, *"Why is everything backwards in Portuguese?"* because it may seem that way many times. Keep your mind open to the many differences that you will find in the language that go far beyond just the words.

Tip #2 - Take Risks

Be fearless. Talk to as many people as you can. The more practice you get the better and don't worry about looking like a fool when you are , which as you will find out can be a common mistake. If anyone is laughing remember they are not laughing at you. Just laugh with them, move on, and LEARN from it, which brings us to our next tip.

Tip #3 - Learn from your Mistakes

It doesn't help to get down because you made one more mistake when trying to order at a restaurant, take a taxi, or just in a friendly conversation. Making mistakes is a HUGE part of learning a language. You have to put yourself out there as we said and be willing to make tons of mistakes! Why? Because what can you do with mistakes. You can LEARN from them. If you never make a mistake, you probably are not learning as much as you could. So every time you mess up when trying to communicate, learn from it, move on, and keep your head up!

Tip #4 - Immerse yourself in the language

If you're not yet able to go to a Portuguese-speaking country, try to pretend that you are. Surround yourself with Portuguese. Listen to music in Portuguese, watch movies, TV shows, in Portuguese. Play games on your phone, computer, etc. in Portuguese. Another great idea is to actually put your phone, computer, tablet and/or other electronic devices in Portuguese. It can be frustrating at first but in the end this exposure will definitely pay off.

Tip #5 - Start Thinking in Portuguese

I remember being a senior in high school and working as a lifeguard at a fairly deserted pool. While I was sitting and staring at the empty waters, I would speak to myself or think to myself (to not seem so crazy) in Portuguese. I would describe my surroundings, talk about what I had done and what I was going to do, etc. While I was riding my bike, I would do the same thing. During any activity when you don't need to talk or think about anything else, keep your brain constantly going in Portuguese to get even more practice in the language. So get ready to turn off the English and jumpstart your Portuguese brain!

Tip #6 - Label your Surroundings/Use Flashcards

When I started to learn Portuguese, I bought an excellent book that included stickers so that you could label your surroundings. So I had stickers all over my parents' house from the kitchen to the bathroom that labeled the door, the dishes, furniture, parts of the house, etc. It was a great, constant reminder of how to say these objects in another language. You can just make your own labels and stick them all over the house and hope it doesn't bother your family or housemates too much!

Tip #7 - Use Context clues, visuals, gestures, expressions, etc.

If you don't understand a word that you have heard or read, look or listen to the surrounding words and the situation to help you. If you are in a restaurant and your friend says, "I am going to ??? a sandwich." You can take a guess that she said *order* or *eat* but you don't have to understand every word in order to understand the general meaning. When you are in a conversation use gestures, expressions, and things around you to help communicate your meaning. Teaching English as a second language to young learners taught me this. If you act everything out, you are more likely to get your point across. If you need to say the word *bird* and you don't know how you can start flapping your arms and chirping and then you will get your point across and possibly learn how to say *bird*. It may seem ridiculous but as I said, you have to be willing to look silly to learn another language and this greatly helps your language communication and learning.

Tip #8 - Circumlocution

Circumlo... what? This is just a fancy word for describing something when you don't know how to say it. If you are looking to buy an umbrella and don't know how to say it, what can you do? You can describe it using words you know. You can say, it is something used for the rain that opens and closes and then hopefully someone will understand you, help you, and maybe teach you how to say this word. Using circumlocution is excellent language practice and is much better than just giving up when you don't know how to say a word. So keep talking even if you have a limited vocabulary. Say what you can and describe or act out what you can't!

SECTION 1: THE BASICS

Chapter 1: Getting the Pronunciation Down

Below I will break down general Portuguese pronunciation of the whole alphabet dividing it into vowels and consonants. You will also find the equivalent sounds from the IPA chart whenever possible, so here's a refresher in case you haven't seen it in a while:

Vowel Sounds		Diphtongs		
iː	ɪ	ʊ	uː	eɪ
			ɪə	
e	ə	ɜː	ɔː	ʊə
			ɔɪ	ə
				ʊ
ae	ʌ	ɑː	ɒ	eə
				aɪ	aʊ

Consonant Sounds						
p	b	t	d	tʃ	dʒ	k	g
f	v	θ	ð	s	z	ʃ	ʒ
m	n	ŋ	h	l	r	w	j

Also, you can visit this website to hear each sound whenever you need to:

http://www.ipachart.com/

This is so important I have separated the paragraph just for it. There are of course some sounds in Portuguese that we never make in English and you possibly have never made in your life, so on the table containing them, I have added example words that you should put on google translate to hear how they are pronounced, please do so, it will make a huge difference in the effectiveness of this chapter!

So get ready to start moving your mouth and tongue in a new way that may seem strange at first, but as I keep saying, practice makes perfect!

One great thing about Portuguese is that the letters almost always stay consistent as far as what sound they make, and you pronounce words the same way you write it. Unlike English in which the vowels can make up to 27 different sounds depending on how they are mixed. Be thankful that you don't have to learn English or at least have already learned English.

The first chart will show you the accents, or special characters that Portuguese has. They are used not only to change intonation of the vowel (we only have them on vowels) but also to tell you which is the stressed syllable in the word.

Accents

Character	Vowels it goes over	Example	Sound
´	Á, é í ó ú	Árvore(tree), é (to be), sílaba(syllable), forró (type of music) and saúde (health)	Long, non nasal: /ɑ:/, /e/, /i:/, /ɔ:/, /ʊ/
`	À	Used to show reference to something, like an arrow pointing	/ɑ:/
^	Â,ê,ô	Âmbar (ember), português (Portuguese), metrô(subway)	/ʌ/, nasal /e/, /ɒ/
~	Ã, õ	Mãe (mother), questões (questions)	/ʌ/ and nasal /ɒ/

The charts on the next page will explain how to say the letter, pronounce it, and if there is an example in an English word of how to say it, I put it in the right column, beside the English example you'll find Portuguese ones:

Vowel Sounds

Vowel	How to say the letter	How to pronounce it in a word	As in…	And in Portuguese:
A	/ɑ:/	ɑ:	T<u>a</u>co	Biciclet<u>a</u> (bike)
E	/e/	/e/	<u>E</u>gg	Flor<u>e</u>sta (forest)
I	/I/	/I/	<u>Easy</u>	Passe<u>i</u>o (go somewhere for leisure)
O	/ɒ/ or /ɔ:/	/ɒ/ or /ɔ:/	<u>O</u>n or f<u>or</u>	P<u>o</u>ça (puddle) or <u>o</u>vo (egg)
U	/ʊ/	/ʊ/	B<u>oo</u>k	H<u>u</u>mano (human)

Consonant Sounds

Consonant	How to say the letter	How to pronounce it in a word	As in…	And in Portuguese:
b	/b/	similar to English /b/	boat	Barco (boat)
c	seh	/k/ before *a, o,* or *u* /s/ before *e* or *i*	cat cereal	Casa (house) Certo (correct)
ch	ceh agah	/ʃ/	shower	Chamar (call over)
d	deh	a soft /d/ (place your tongue at the back of your upper teeth)	day	Dente (tooth)
f	efe	/f/	free	Fácil (easy)
g	ge	/g/ before *a, o* and *u* /ʒ/ before *e* and *i*	Go vision	Grande (big) Viagem (trip)
h	aga	Silent when not with consonants	honest	Homem (man)
j	ʒota	/ʒ/	vision	Jogo (game)
k	kah	/k/	karaoke	Only found in foreign words
l	ele	/l/ in the beginning of words and like English ʊ/ in the end o them	Look and Book	Legal (cool as in something nice)
ll	ele ele	Same as /l/		
M	eme	/m/	money	It should always come before p and b, embora (although)
N	ene	/n/	no	Portuguese words never end in n, Nariz (nose)
Nh	ene aga	/ɲ/	canyon	Sonho (dream)
p	peh	like English /p/ but you don't aspirate	panda	Padaria (backery)
Q	keh	/k/ (q is always followed by u like in English)	quilt	Quieto (quiet)

Consonants continued

Consonant	How to say the letter	How to pronounce it in a word	As in…	And in Portuguese:
R	ehe	* in the beginning of words or between a consonant ad a vowel it sounds like /h/ * between two vowels it sounds like a rhotic /r/	Hotel No example in English	Rosa (rose or the color pink) Caro (expensive)
rr	erre	Sounds like /h/	hotel	Carro (car)
S	Esse	*At he beginning of words like /s/ *Between vogals /z/	Sorry zoo	Sábado (saturday) Casamento (wedding or marriage)
ss	Esse esse	/s/	sorry	Sucesso (success)
T	teh	a soft English /t/, the tongue touches the back of the upper teeth	table	Tamanho (size)
V	veh	/v/	vast	Violão (acoustic guitar)
w	dabliu	Like English w and sometimes like /v/	water	Only foreign words and some names
x	shis	In the beginning or words: /ʃ/, like shower; Between vowels: /z/, like zoo ; or /ks/, like fix ; or /s/, like sorry .	shower zoo fix sorry	/ʃ/: Xarope (syrup) /z/: exame (exam) /ks/: fixo (unmoving/unchanging) /s/: máximo (maximun)

y	ípsilon	like English y	yellow	Only foreign words and names
z	zê	/z/	zoo	Zangado (angry)

Special Leters

ç	sedilha	Like /s/	Summer
lh	Ele aga	/ʎ/ - It sounds similar to /l//l/	No similar in English, please use google translator to hear "palha"

Note: If you're not sure how to pronounce a word, please type it in *Google translate* then click on the little speaker icon in the bottom left corner to hear the correct pronunciation.

Chapter 2: Portuguese and English differences and Basic Grammar

We will now start with the most basic. I will explain some major things that are different between English and Portuguese and some general Portuguese grammar rules. Along with this, I will include basic vocabulary such as question words, numbers, colors, and other useful words and phrases to give you a foundation to help support you through the rest of this book. If you are trying to answer the practice questions in the following chapters and don't know how to say a vocabulary word, you will most likely find it in this chapter.

Differences between English and Portuguese

1. **Masculine and Feminine Words:** In Portuguese there are words that are feminine and masculine. It has nothing to do with the actual word. For example the word *dress* (vestido) is masculine and the word *beard* (a barba) is feminine. Also, as a general rule, nouns that end in *a* are feminine and nouns that end in *o* are masculine.

2. **Word Order:** The word order is often different from English. For example, the adjective goes after the noun. Instead of the *red car*, it is the *car red* (carro vermelho). You should also remember that in Portuguese the word order doesn't change when asking questions, all you have to do is say the sentence with a question intonation.

3. **Adjective and Noun Agreement:** The adjectives must agree with the gender (feminine or masculine) and the number (singular or plural). For example, the red cars (os carros vermelhos or the black cat (o gato preto)

4. **Second person:** There are two ways of saying you, você and tu, they are used in different regions of Brazil (mostly in the southern region), and they change verbs differently as you will see in the grammar part.

5. **Verb Changes:** Portuguese has more verb changes, the verb run changes 5 times in the present tense. I run (eu corro) you run (você corre/tu corres) he or she runs (corre) we run (corremos) they or you all run (correm). For this reason, Portuguese also uses personal pronouns much less as I will mention in number 5.

6. **Lack of Pronoun (I, he, she, we, it, they, etc.) Use:** Because of the   verb changes mentioned in   number 4, you do not have to use   pronouns as

often. Instead of saying você corre/tu corres,(you run) you can just say *corre* because we already know that it is you who we are talking about from the verb.

7.Word Endings: Diminutives are very commonly added to words especially the diminutive 'inho' which is used to say something in a cuter way or to talk about something that is a small. For example, "the cute little dog" (o cachorrinho) but it is used much more frequently than in English and can be added to adjectives and nouns.

8. Lack of Capitalization: Many words that are capitalized in English are not in Portuguese. For example, days of the week, months, languages and nationalities.

Egg: Tuesday = terça-feira
February = fevereiro
Portuguese = português
Canadian = canadense

9. Age: In Portuguese you aren't x years old, you have X years: Eu tenho 23 anos.

10. To have for eating: In Portuguese you can't say you have/had a meal you have to say the actual verb.

Egg: I had lunch = Eu almocei
I had a cheese sandwish = Eu comi um sanduíche.
I had fruit for breakfast = Eu comi frutas no café da manhã

Basic Grammar

The four ways of saying *the* and the four ways of saying *a* in Portuguese are listed below

Portuguese Articles

The	Masculine	Feminine
Singular	o	a
Plural	os	as

a	Masculine	Feminine
Singular	Um	Uma
Plural	Uns	umas

Note: 'o,' 'a,' 'os,' and 'as' all mean 'the' in English. However, remember you have to agree them with the gender and number of the noun.

Ex: o gato / a gata ---> the cat
Um gato / uma gata ---> a cat

a pessoa ---> the person
uma pessoa ---> a person

os cachorros / as cachorras ---> the dogs
uns cachorros / umas cachorras ---> some dogs

as guitarras ---> the electric guitars
uma guitarra ---> an electric guitar

Note: The articles are used much more frequently in Portuguese.

Personal Pronouns

I	Eu
you	Você/tu
he, she	ele, ela,
We	Nós
They	Eles (masculine), Elas (feminine)

*As mentioned before, personal pronouns are not used as much in Portuguese

Question Words

What?	Quê?
Where?	Onde?
When?	Quando?
Which?	Qual?
Why?	Por que?
Who?	Quem?

Numbers 1-10

1	Um

2	dois
3	três
4	quatro
5	cinco
6	seis
7	sete
8	oito
9	nove
10	dez

Numbers 11-20

11	onze
12	doze
13	treze
14	catorze
15	quinze
16	desesseis
17	desessete
18	dezoito
19	dezenove
20	vinte

*For 21-29 it follows this pattern: vinte +e+ number as one word

Ex: 21 ---> vinte e um, 22 ---> vinte e dois, 23 ---> vinte e três, etc.

Numbers 30-100+

30	trinta
40	quarenta
50	Cinquenta
60	sessenta
70	setenta
80	oitenta
90	noventa
100	Cem
105	Cento e cinco
115	Cento e quinze

*For 31-99 it follows this pattern: trinta +e+ number

Ex:

33 = trinta e três
45 = quarenta e cinco
78 = setenta e oito,

* For 101 to 199, just say cento +e+ the number
Ex: 190= cento e noventa (see examples above)

Numbers 200-1000

200	duzentos
300	trezentos
400	quatrocentos
500	quinhentos
600	seiscentos
700	setecentos
800	oitocentos
900	novecentos
1000	mil

Colors

Red	Vermelho/a
Orange	Laranja
Yellow	Amarelo/a
Green	Verde
Blue	Azul
Purple	Roxo/a
Pink	Rosa
Black	Preto/a
White	Branco/a
Brown	Marrom
Gray	Cinza

Other useful vocabulary and phrases

Yes	Sim
No	não
But	Mas
also/too	Também
Is	é (permanent) está (temporary)
And	E
An	um (masculine) uma (feminine)
In	Em
With	Com
Or	Ou
Now	agora
because	porque
Well	então/assim
Sorry	Me desculpe
excuse me	Com licença
thank you	Obrigado/a (men say obrigado, women say obrigada)
you're welcome	de nada
Please	por favor
me too.	eu também
Very	Muito
A lot	Muito
That's okay/Okay	Está bem /Tá bom

Chapter 3: Greetings, Introductions, and Other Useful Phrases

Como vai? Tudo bem?

In this chapter we will go over the very necessary ways to greet and introduce yourself to others. We have to remember that there are two different ways of saying *you* in Portuguese- você and tu. I remember often worrying about when to use one or the other. If you are unsure you can just go with você as it is the more modern speech. Below is a list of common greetings in Portuguese.

Common Greetings

Hello	Oi/ Olá
Good Morning	Bom dia
Good Afternoon	Boa Tarde
Good evening/Good night	Boa Noite
General Greeting	Bom dia

Asking and Answering 'How are you?'

How are you?	Como vai?/ Tudo bem?
How are you doing?	Como vão as coisas?
Well/Very well	Bem/ muito bem/tudo bem
Good and you? (informal)	Tudo bem e você?
So-so	Mais ou menos
What's up? What's new?	O que há de novo? O que foi?

Saying Goodbye

English	Portuguese
Goodbye	Tchau
See you later	Até mais/até a próxima
See you tomorrow	Até amanhã/até
See you soon	Nos vemos em breve/ até mais
See you	Nos vemos/ a gente se vê
Bye	Tchau-tchau

Exercícios!

Translate the following conversation into English

#1

- Oi Pedro! ----->

- Bom dia Ana! ----->

- Como vai? ----->

- Muito bem, obrigado, e você? ----->

- Estou ótimo, obrigado. ----->

- Até mais, Ana. ----->

- Nos vemos, Pedro! ----->

*Did you notice there were some words that were not listed in the vocabulary above? Were you still able to use context clues and/or cognates (words that sound similar in both languages) and fill in the rest of the meaning as is suggested in the introduction? Remember, it is a great skill to have because most of the time there will be words that you may not understand in a conversation.

Introductions and Other phrases

What is your name? (informal)	Como você se chama? Qual seu nome?
My name is…	Me chamo…/Meu nome é
Nice to meet you!	Prazer em conhecê-lo
It's a pleasure.	É um prazer.
Me too.	Eu também
Where are you from?	De onde você é?
I am from the U.S.	Sou dos Estados Unidos.
How old are you?	Quantos anos você tem?
I am… years old.	Tenho … anos.
Canada	Canadá
England	Inglaterra
South Africa	África do Sul

Australia	Austrália

Cultural Note: **Kissing** ---In Portuguese speaking countries, people usually greet with a kiss on one cheek (southern Brazil), or both cheeks (southeast), or "três para casar" three so you'll get married

*Below, I will list some useful phrases for when you don't understand, are confused, and need some clarification: a very common occurrence when learning a language.

Other Useful Phrases

I don't understand.	Não entendi.
Can you repeat, please.	Você pode repetir, por favor?
Speak more slowly, please.	Fala mais devagar, por favor.
How do you say …?	Como se diz/fala…?
What does this mean?	O que significa isso?
What is this?	O que é isso?
Can you help me?	Você pode me ajudar?
Do you speak English?	Você fala inglês?
I speak a little Portuguese.	Eu falo um pouco de português.
I don't know.	Não sei.
Write it down, please.	escreve por favor.

Exercícios!

Translate the following conversation into English

#2

- Boa tarde! ----->

- Eai! Como vai? ----->

- Bem, obrigado, e você? ----->

- Mais ou menos. ----->

- Qual seu nome? ----->

- Me chamo Adriana, e você, como se chama? ----->

- Meu nome é Alberto. ----->

- Quantos anos você tem? ----->

- Tenho 25 anos e você? ----->

- Tenho 29 anos. De onde você é? ----->

- Sou do Canadá. De onde você é? ----->

- Sou da Colômbia. ----->

- Muito prazer! ----->

- O prazer é meu! ----->

Match the Phrases
1. I speak a little Portuguese------------------------------a. O que é isto?
2. Write it down, please. -----------------------------b. Não entendi
3. Do you speak English? ----------------------------c. Falo um pouco de Português.
4. I don't understand. -------------------------------d. Não sei
5. How do you say…?--------------------------------e. Fala mais devagar por favor.
6. I don't know. -------------------------------------f. O que significa isso?
7. Speak slowly please. -----------------------------g. Escreve por favor.
8. Can you repeat, please? ------------------------h. Fala inglês?
9. What is this? ------------------------------------i. Como se diz…?
10. What does this mean? -------------------------j. Pode repetir, por favor?

Chapter 3 Answers

Translation #1
- Oi Pedro!
- Bom dia Ana!
- Como vai?
- Muito bem, obrigado, e você?
- Estou ótimo, obrigado.
- Até mais, Ana.
- Nos vemos, Pedro!

- Hi Pedro!
- Good morning, Ana!
- How's it going?
- Very good, thanks. And you?
- Excellent, thanks.
- See you later, Ana.
- See you, Pedro!

Translation #2

- Boa tarde!
- Eai! Como vai?
- Bem, obrigado, e você?
- Mais ou menos.
- Qual seu nome?
- Me chamo Adriana, e você, como se chama?
- Meu nome é Alberto.
- Quantos anos você tem?
- Tenho 25 anos e você?
- Tenho 29 anos. De onde você é?
- Sou do Canadá. De onde você é?
- Sou da Colômbia.
- Muito prazer!
- É um prazer para mim também!

- Good afternoon!
- Hi! How are you?
- Good, thanks. And you?
- So so, thank you.
- What's your name?

- My name is Adriana, And you what is your name?
- My name is Alberto.
- How old are you?
- I am 25 years old and you?
- I'm 29 years old. Where are you from?
- I am from Canada. Where are you from?
- I am from Colombia
- Nice to meet you!
- It's a pleasure for me too!

Match the Phrases
1. I speak a little Portuguese. -----------c. Falo um pouco de Português
2. Write it down, please. ------------g. Escreve por favor.
3. Do you speak English?   -----------h. Fala inglês?
4. I don't understand. ---------------b. Não entendi.
5. How do you say…?----------------i. Como se diz…?
6. I don't know. -----------------------d. Não sei.
7. Speak slowly please.--------------e. Fala mais devagar por favor.
8. Can you repeat, please?---------j. Pode repetir, por favor?
9. What is this?----------------------a. O que é isto?
10. What does this mean? ----------f. O que significa isto?

Chapter 4: About Time - Telling time, Days of Week, Dates

In this chapter, I will discuss how to talk about time, telling time, days of week, months, etc. Something to remember about Latin-American cultures is that time is much more relaxed. When you are invited to a gathering with friends, it is acceptable to show up a couple of hours late. I remember when I studied in Chile, most of the students who showed up to class on time, were foreigners. The Chilean students usually would file in 15 to 30 minutes late. I also recall going to an interview in the Dominican Republic and showing up 15 minutes early as one should. I ended up waiting for over an hour until the interview started. Typically with business and school, time is stricter, but not always as my experience has taught me. Below I have several useful phrases to talk about time. Also, keep in mind the the time is based on the 24h clock.

Telling Time

What time is is?	Que horas são?
It's one.	É uma hora.
It's two.	São… horas (são is used for all times except 12h, 00h, 01h and 13h)
It's four thirty.	São quatro e meia.
It's fifteen until eight.	São quinze para as oito.
From about 06h to 11h (in the morning)	Da manhã
12h to about 18h (in the afternoon)	Da tarde
19h to 00h (at night)	Da noite
From about 01h to 05h (early morning)	Da madrugada

* **If you want to add minutes to the hour just use the word 'e'**

    Ex: It is 6:05 = São seis e cinco

Now you try:

1. It is 3:05 _____

2. It is 10:45 _____

3. It is 8:20 _____

***If you want to say that it is 15 til, 10 til, or 5 til an hour, use the following format:**

It is five minus ten (It is ten til five) = São dez para as cinco
It is eleven minus 15 (15 til noon) = São quinze para o meio dia (meia noite for 12am)

Now you try:

4. It is fifteen til three_____
5. It is five til seven _____
6. It is ten til nine_____

Days of the Week

What day is today?	Que dia é hoje?
Today is Thursday	Hoje é quinta
Today	Hoje
Yesterday	Ontem
Tomorrow	Amanhã
Monday	segunda-feira
Tuesday	terça-feira
Wednesday	quarta-feira
Thursday	quinta-feira
Friday	sexta-feira
Saturday	sábado
Sunday	domingo

* As mentioned before, Portuguese does not typically capitalize the days of the weeks.
* Also, when you are saying *On Monday I'm going to the doctor* ---> *Na segunda vou ao médico* (you usually only say the day of the week without the "–feira")

Talking about the Date

What is the date today?	Qual é a data de hoje?
Today is February 15th	Hoje é quinze de fevereiro

January	janeiro
February	fevereiro
March	março
April	abril
May	maio
June	junho
July	julho
August	agosto
September	setembro
October	outubro
November	novembro
December	dezembro

*Date format

É dia (#) de month

É dia <u>quinze</u> de <u>junho.</u> = It is June 15th

Exercícios!

Choose the correct answer

7. Que horas são?

a. São uma da tarde ----------------------b. São um da tarde

c. É uma da tarde ---------------------- d. É um do tarde

8. Hoje é sexta .

a. Today is Monday ---------------------- b. Today is Friday

c. Today is Sunday ---------------------- d. Today is Thursday.

9. Today is March 27th

a. Hoje é dia 27 de março ---------------------- b. Hoje é março 27

c. Hoje é 27 de março ---------------------- d. Hoje é o março 27

10. It is ten til seven

a. São sete para as dez ---------------------- b. São sete menos dez

c. São dez para as sete ---------------------- d. É dez sete para as dez

11. It is 15:45 (3:45 pm)

a. É três e quinze ---------------------- b. São quinze e três

c. São três e quinze ----------------------d. São quinze e quarenta e cinco

Chapter 4 Answers

1. It is 3:05 ----> São três e cinco.

2. It is 10:45 ----> São dez e quarenta e cinco ou São quinze para as onze.

3. It is 8:20 ----> São oito e vinte.

4. It is fifteen til three. ----> São quinze para as três.

5. It is five til seven. ----> São cinco para as sete.

6. It is ten til nine. ----> São dez para as nove.

Choose the correct answer

7. Que horas são?

c. É uma da tarde

8. Hoje é sexta.

b. Today is Friday.

9. Today is March 27th

a. Hoje é dia 27 de março

10. It is ten til seven

c. São dez para as sete

11. It is 15:45 (3:45 pm)

d. São quinze e quarenta e cinco

Chapter 5: How Do You Like This Weather?

Como está o tempo?

This chapter will discuss how to talk about the weather, something people often talk about when there is nothing else to talk about. It also is useful information to have, as in some Portuguese-speaking countries, it can be perfectly sunny one moment and then torrentially raining, the next. Another reminder that languages rarely will translate word for word. For instance, the words for weather and climate are "tempo" and "clima" respectively, so when someone asks "como está o tempo" remember they mean the wheather and not what time it is. Below are some useful phrases and vocabulary to use when talking about the weather.

Weather Expressions

What's the weather like today?	Como está o tempo hoje?
It is cold	Está frio
It is hot	Está quente
It is sunny	Está sol
It is windy	Está ventando
The weather is nice	Está bom
The weather is bad	Está ruim
It's cool.	Está fresquinho
It's raining.	Está chovendo
Is it going to rain today?	Vai chover hoje?
Yes, it's going to rain, No, it's not going to rain	Sim, vai chover/Não, não vai chover
It's snowing	Está nevando
Really?	Sério?

* **If you want to say: It is very hot, cold, etc. you must use *muito***

Ex: It is very hot ----> Está muito quente

It is very cold ----> Está muito frio, etc.

Exercícios!

Choose the correct answer

1. Como está o tempo hoje? (this one has two possibilities)

a. Está muito quente ----------------- b. Está muito calor

c. Está fazendo muito calor ----------------- d. Fazendo muito quente

2. It is very sunny today. (this one has two possibilities)

a. Está muito ensolarado hoje ----------------- b. É muito sol hoje.

c. Tem muito sol hoje. ----------------- d. Tem muitos sois hoje.

3. Vai chover hoje?

a. Não, não chover hoje ----------------- b. Sim, vai chover hoje

c. Sim hoje chove ----------------- d. Não não choverá hoje

Translate to Portuguese

- Hi friend, how are you?

- Good! How is the weather today?

- It's nice! It's not going to rain.

- But, it is very windy.

- Yes, but very sunny too.

- See you tomorrow!

- Goodbye!

Chapter 5 Answers

Choose the correct answer

1. Como está o tempo hoje?

a. Está muito quente and c. Está fazendo muito calor

2. It is very sunny today.

a. Está muito ensolarado hoje and c. Tem muito sol hoje.

3. Vai chover hoje?

b. Sim, vai chover hoje.

Translation

- Hi friend, how are you?
- Good! How is the weather today?
- It's nice! It's not going to rain.
- But, it is very windy.
- Yes, but very sunny too.
- See you tomorrow!
- Goodbye!

- Oi amigo/amiga, como vai?
- Bem! Como está o tempo hoje?
- Está ótimo! Não vai chover.
- Mas está ventando muito.
- Sim, mas também está muito ensolarado.
- Até amanhã!
- Tchau!

SECTION 2: IN THE CITY AND TRAVELLING

Chapter 6: Directions

Onde fica o banco?

Now, we will move onto some more very useful everyday vocabulary, especially if you are in a new country and have no idea where anything is. Now, these days with google maps and GPS, stopping to ask for directions is less common. However, in many Portuguese-speaking countries, you will not have such easy access to internet while you are on the streets at least. So get ready to have to actually talk to people face to face and maybe occasionally get a little lost. More importantly, be prepared to pay attention to your sorroundings, and take precautions like:

- Don't speak on your phone in the streets, duck into a restaurant or other commercial establishments, that's also usual for Brazilians. Don't wear jewelry when walking around or going to places like the beach and parks.

- Don't flaunt your amazing photo camera around! And please, PLEASE, don't hang it around your neck when walking around!

Below I have some of the most useful phrases and vocabulary for getting around in Portuguese.

Phrases to talk about Directions

Where is it?	Onde fica?
Excuse me, where is the…	Por favor, onde fica a/o…
It's next to the…	Fica do lado da/do…
It's in front of the…	Fica na frente da/do …
Keep straight	Sigue em frente/toda vida…
Turn right	Vira à direita
Turn left	Vira à esquerda
It's on the right/left	Fica no lado direito/ esquerdo
Far from	Longe de/da/do
Near to	Perto de/da/do
Above	Em cima de/da/do
Below	Embaixo
Behind	Atrás de/da/do

* Notice the contraction:

Places

The bank	o banco
The restaurant	o restaurante
The post office	os correios
The supermarket	o supermercado
The pharmacy	a farmácia
The bakery	a padaria
Bus/Train station	Ponto de Ônibus/Trem
Store	Loja
Church	Igreja
Stationary Store	Papelaria

*Did you notice which words are masculine and feminine?

Notice the difference: It is next to the bank = Fica do lado **do** banco.

It is next to the store = Fica do lado **da** loja.

Other Phrases

I am lost.	Estou perdido/perdida
How do I get to …?	Como chego na/no …?
Cross the street.	Atravessa a rua.
Where am I now?	Onde estou agora?
the corner	a esquina
one block	Um quarteirão
street	Rua
here	Aqui
there	Ali
there	lá (farther away)

Time Expressions

Before	Antes
Now	Agora
After	Depois
Later/Then	Mais tarde/então

Exercícios!

Choose the correct answer

1. The bank is next to the post office.

a. O banco fica do lado dos correios.----- b. O banco fica na frente dos correios.

c. O banco fica do lado da correios.   .----- d. A banco fica do lado do correios.

2. Turn right at the bakery.

a. Vire à direita na loja.----- b. Vire à direita no banco.

c. Vire à direita na padaria. .----- d. Vire à esquerda na loja.

3. The store is close to the church.

a. A praia fica perto da igreja.----- b. A loja fica na frente da igreja.

c. Os correios ficam perto da igreja.----- d. A loja fica perto da igreja.

Translate to English

- Por favor, onde fica o ponto de ônibus?

- Segue reto e vira a direita na esquina.

- Ok.

- Depois anda três quarteirões.

- Ok

- E atravessa a rua, fica do lado da padaria.

- É muito longe?

- Não, não é muito longe.

- Muito obrigada senhor!

- De nada, até mais.

Chapter 6 Answers

Choose the correct answer

1. The bank is next to the post office.

a. O banco fica do lado dos correios

2. Turn right at the bakery.

c. Vire à direita na padaria.

3. The store is close to the church.

d. A loja fica perto da igreja

Translation

- Por favor, onde fica o ponto de ônibus?
- Segue reto e vira a direita na esquina.
- Ok.
- Depois anda três quarteirões.
- Ok
- E atravessa a rua, fica do lado da padaria.
- É muito longe?
- Não, não é muito longe.
- Muito obrigada senhor!
- De nada, até mais.

- Excuse me, where is the bus station?
- Keep straight and turn left at the corner y dobla a la izquierda en la esquina.
- Ok.
- Then, keep going for three blocks.
- Ok
- and cross the Street and it's next to the stationary store
- Is it very far?
- No, it's not very far.
- Well, thank you sir!
- Your welcome, see you later.

Chapter 7: Shopping

Quanto custa isso?

Now, let's move onto a very enjoyable (usually) and common activity that we do in other countries- shopping! Whether it be shopping for cheesy souvenirs for your friends and family or shopping for some stylish local clothes for yourself, we've got the basics to help you bargain around and hopefully find what you are looking for. Remember that bargaining can be a big part of shopping in the markets of most Portuguese-speaking countries. If you don't do it, you definitely will get taken advantage of by some lucky shopkeepers who see the 'gringos' coming from a mile away. So, let's see if we can find you a great deal!

Shopping phrases

How can I help you?	Como posso te ajudar?
How much does it cost?	Quanto custa?
How much is it?	Quanto é?
Which one do you want?	Qual você quer?
I would like that one.	Quero esse (masculine) essa (feminine)
It's too expensive	Está muito caro
Do you have…?	Você tem …?
Do you have bigger/smaller?	Tem tamanho maior/menor?
Do you accept credit cards?	Aceita cartão de crédito?
We only accept cash.	Só aceitamos dinheiro.
Can I try it on?	Pode experimentar?
I'm just looking.	Só estou olhando.
Of course!	Claro!

Shopping Vocabulary

souvenirs	As lembrancinhas
clothes	a roupa
shirt	a camisa/blusa
pants	As calças
shorts	os shorts
a dress	um vestido
a jacket	uma jaqueta

shoes	os sapatos
cap	O bone
keychain	o chaveiro

* Note that you say *um/uma* for *a* and it has to match the gender of the word.
Ex: umn vestido = a dress
uma camisa =a shirt

Below, I will list the demonstrative adjectives in Portuguese (this, that, these, those) as they are very useful to use when shopping, 'I would like that one, please.'

Demonstrative Adjectives (This, That, These, Those)

*Note: These also change according to gender and number

This and That

English	Masculine	Feminine	Gender Neutral (Only used for things! Never for living beings)
This	Esse	Essa	Isso
That	Aquele	Aquela	Aquilo

These and Those

English	Masculine	Feminine
These	Esses	Essas
Those	Aqueles	Aquelas

* If you want to say: *that shirt*, remember to match 'that' to the word shirt.

Ex: ess**a** chaquet**a** = that

ess**e** gorr**o** = that

est**as** camis**as** = these

ess**es** chaveir**os** = these key chains

Exercícios!

Choose the correct answer

1. Camisetas

a. Essa.-----b. Essas

c. Esse .-----d. Esses

2. I would like to try on these shoes.

a. Eu gostaria de experimentar esses sapatos .----- b. Eu gostar de experimentar esses sapatos .
c. Eu gostaria de experimentar essa sapatos .----- d. Eu gostaria de experimentar esse sapatos .

3. Would you like to buy this jacket?

a. Você gostaria de levar esse jaqueta?----- b. Você gostaria de levar aquela jaqueta?
c. Você gostaria de levar essa jaqueta?----- d. Você gostaria de levar essas jaqueta?

Translate to English

- Bom dia, em que posso ajudá-lo?

- Só estou olhando, obrigado.

- De nada.

- Quanto é esse vestido?

- Duzentos reais.

- Está muito caro! E essas calças?

- Cento e cinquenta reais.

- Posso experimentar?

- Claro!

- Vocês aceitam cartão de crédito?

- Não, só aceitamos dinheiro.

- Está bem, muito obrigada.

Chapter 7 Answers

Choose the correct answer

1. Camisetas

b. Essas

2. I would like to try on these shoes.

a. Eu gostaria de experimentar esses sapatos .

3. Would you like to buy this jacket?

c. Você gostaria de levar essa jaqueta?

Translation

- Bom dia, em que posso ajudá-lo?
- Só estou olhando, obrigado.
- De nada.
- Quanto é esse vestido?
- Duzentos reais.
- Está muito caro! E essas calças?
- Cento e cinquenta reais.
- Posso experimentar?
- Claro!
- Vocês aceitam cartão de crédito?
- Não, só aceitamos dinheiro.
- Está bem, muito obrigada.

- Good morning, how can I help you?
- I'm just looking, thanks.
- Your welcome.
- How much does this dress cost?
- 200 pesos.
- It's very expensive! And these pants?
- 150 pesos.
- Can I try them on?
- Of course!
- Do you accept credit cards?

- No, we only accept cash.
- Okay, thank you very much.

Chapter 8: Going out to eat

Eu gostaria de comer...

In this chapter we will discuss another common and delicious activity- going out to eat in restaurants. Some cultural suggestions for going out to eat could be to not expect the same type of service that you get back home. I Brazil you don't tip the waiter, most places will add 10% to your check and it is up to you to choose to pay it or not, the vast majority of Brazilians always pays it, it is only when service is really really bad that we don't. You also may have to specify if you want your water carbonated (com gás) or regular (sem gás) literally water with or without gas. Let's get ready to eat! Bon Appetite or as they say in Portuguese, *Bom apetite!*

Restaurant phrases

What would you like?	O que vocês gostariam?
I would like to eat...	Eu gostaria de comer...
I would like to drink...	Eu gostaria de beber...
Menu, please	O menu, por favor
What do you recommend?	O que você recomenda?
Can you bring me?	Poderia me trazer...
Excuse me, sir	Com licença, senhor
Excuse me, ma'am	Com licença, senhora Com licença, moça (younger)
Drink	A bebida
A glass	Um copo
Soft Drink	Refrigerante
Juice	Suco
A glass of water	Um copo de água
A beer	Uma cerveja
A glass of wine	Uma taça de vinho
Dessert	A sobremesa
Tip	A gorjeta
check, please	a conta, por favor
So/then	Então

Food Vocabulary

What does this dish have?	O que tem nesse prato?
Does this dish have…?	Esse prato tem…?
Meat (used to refer to beef and pork)	A carne
Fish	O peixe
Chicken	O frango
Ham	O presunto
Egg	O ovo
Pasta	O macarrão
Salad	A salada
Bread	O pão
Cheese	O queijo
Vegetables	As verduras
Breakfast	Café da manhã
Lunch	Almoço
Dinner	Jantar
There is/there are/includes	Tem/Têm/inclui

*A very useful verb, **tem= There is/There are**.

Ex: Tem muito pão e queijo = There is a lot of bread and cheese.
Têm sanduíches de presunto para o almoço.= There are ham sandwiches for lunch.

Exercícios!

Choose the correct answer

1. This dish has fish, vegetables, and bread.

a. Este prato tem peixe, verduras e pão.

b. Este prato tem peixe, carne e pão.

c. Este prato tem queijo, frango e pão.

d. Este prato tem presunto, salada e pão.

2. Can you bring me a beer please?

a. Por favor, você pode me trazer uma cerveja?

b. Por favor, você pode me trazer um suco?

c. Por favor, você pode me trazer um cerveja?

d. Por favor, você pode trazer uma cerveja para ele?

3. Excuse me ma'am, the check please.

a. Com licença moço, pode trazer a conta por favor?

b. Com licença senhor, pode trazer a conta por favor?

c. Com licença senhora, pode trazer a conta por favor?

d. Com licença moça, pode trazer a conta por favor?

4. Para o café da manhã tem pão, queijo e ovos.

a. For lunch there is bread, cheese, and eggs.

b. For breakfast, there is fish, ham, and eggs.

c. For breakfast there is bread, cheese, and eggs.

d. For dinner there is ham, eggs, and bread.

5. Eu gostaria de comer sobremesa depois do jantar.

a. I would like dessert after lunch,

b. I would like dessert after dinner.

c. I would like wine after dinner.

d. I would like dessert after breakfast.

Translate to English

- Boa noite. O que você gostaria?

- Boa noite, o que você recomenda?

- Este prato tem carne, verduras e pão, e é muito gostoso.

- Está bem, eu gostaria de pedir esse prato então.

- E para beber?

- Uma taça de vinho, por favor.

- OK.

- Obrigado.

Chapter 8 Answers

Choose the correct answer

1. This dish has fish, vegetables, and bread.

a. Este prato tem peixe, verduras e pão.

2. Can you bring me a beer please?

a. Por favor, você pode me trazer uma cerveja?

3. Excuse me ma'am, the check please.

c. Com licença senhora, pode trazer a conta por favor?

4. Para o café da manhã tem pão, queijo e ovos.

c. For breakfast there is bread, cheese, and eggs.

5. Eu gostaria de comer sobremesa depois do jantar.

b. I would like dessert after dinner.

Translate to English

- Boa noite. O que você gostaria?
- Boa noite, o que você recomenda?
- Este prato tem carne, verduras e pão, e é muito gostoso.
- Está bem, eu gostaria de pedir esse prato então.
- E para beber?
- Uma taça de vinho, por favor.
- OK.
- Obrigado.

- Good evening. What can I bring you?
- Good evening, what can you recommend?
- This dish has meat, vegetables, and bread and is very delicious.
- Okay, I would like that dish then.
- And to drink?
- A glass of wine please.

- Okay.
- Thank you.

Chapter 9: Going to the Doctor

O que você está sentindo?

Let's talk about a not so fun but absolutely necessary event that you should be prepared for, going to the doctor or the hospital. Getting sick is no fun and even more difficult to deal with when you don't know how to communicate how you are feeling or what is wrong with you. It also can be a very likely event when you are in another country as you are eating food and are exposed to germs both of which your body is not used to. I remember living in Chile and becoming very ill after eating a traditional Chilean dish that is cooked in the ground and includes a mix of shellfish, meats, and sausages. I was taken to the hospital and would have definitely found the following phrases to be very useful. Below are some very basic and useful phrases to use when you are sick, going to the doctor, or hospital.

Phrases to use at the Doctor

What's wrong?	Qual é o problema?
What are you feeling?	O que você está sentindo?
I am sick.	Estou doente.
I have a cold.	Estou resfriado/a.
I have a headache..	Estou com dor de cabeça.
Sore throat	Dor de garganta.
You should rest.	Você deve descansar.
Injection	a injeção
Cough	A tosse
Fever	a febre
Medicine	Remédio/medicação
Prescription	a receita
Here is ...	Aqui está
Do you have health insurance?	Você tem seguro saúde?

*Remember the gender! *Resfriado* and *resfriada* along with many other adjectives have to agree with the gender:

If you are a male = Estou resfriad**o**

If you are a female = Estou resfriad**a**

More Doctor Visit Vocabulary

Where does it hurt?	Onde está doendo?
It hurts here.	Está doendo aqui./Estou com dor aqui
My … hurts.	Meu/minha …está doendo
Head	a cabeça
Arm	O braço
Leg	A perna
Stomach	o estômago
Hand	a mão
Foot	O pé
Eyes	Os olhos
Nose	O nariz
Mouth	a boca
Ear/Inner ear	a orelha/o ouvido
Chest	O peito
I have diarrhea	Estou com diarréia
I have been vomiting	Tenho vomitado

*When you want to talk about something that hurts

My leg hurts= Minha perna está doendo.

His/her head hurts= A cabeça dele/dela está doendo

Does your hand hurt = A sua mão dói?

Exercícios!

Fill in the blanks.

1. His arm hurts.

_____ está doendo

2. My foot hurts.

Meu pé _____

3. Does your head hurt?

A sua_____ está doendo?

4. Her chest hurts.

Ela está com dor_____.

5. Where does it hurt?

Onde está_____?

Match the Vocabulary

1. arm -----------------------a. o estômago
2. chest---------------------b. a boca
3. foot -----------------------c. a cabeça
4. hand----------------------d. o pé
5. ear------------------------e. o braço
6. eyes----------------------f. a mão
7. leg------------------------g. a orelha
8. mouth--------------------h. a perna
9. stomach------------------i. os olhos
10. head--------------------j. o peito

Translate to English

- Boa tarde, o que você está sentindo?

- Estou resfriada e com dor de cabeça.

- Está com dor na garganta?

- Sim, estou com tosse e um pouco de dor de garganta.

- Você não está com febre. Aqui está a receita.

- Obrigado.

- Você tem seguro saúde?

- Sim, tenho.

- Está bem. Descanse bastante e tome bastante água.

- Sim senhor, muito obrigada.

- De nada, tenha um bom dia.

Chapter 9 Answers

Fill in the blanks.

1. His arm hurts.

O braço dele está doendo

2. My foot hurts.

Meu pé está doendo

3. Does your head hurt?

A sua cabeça está doendo?

4. Her chest hurts.

Ela está com dor no peito.

5. Where does it hurt?

Onde está doendo?

Match the Vocabulary

1. arm ----- e. o braço

2. chest----- j. o peito

3. Foot----- d. o pé

4. hand ----- f. a mão

5. ear--------g. a orelha

6. eyes----- i. os olhos

7. leg-------h. a perna

8. mouth------ b. la boca

9. stomach----- a. o estômago

10. head----- c. a cabeça

Translate to English

- Boa tarde, o que você está sentindo?
- Estou resfriada e com dor de cabeça.
- Está com tosse ou dor de garganta?
- Sim, estou com tosse e um pouco de dor de garganta.
- Você não está com febre. Aqui está a receita.
- Obrigado.
- Você tem seguro saúde?
- Sim, tenho.
- Está bem. Descanse bastante e tome bastante água.
- Sim senhor, muito obrigada.
- De nada, melhoras.

- Good afternoon, what are you feeling?
- I have a cold and headache.
- Do you have a cough or sore throat?
- Yes I have a cough and a little bit of a sore throat.
- You don't have a fever. Here is a prescription.
- Thank you.
- Do you have health insurance?
- Yes, I do.
- Okay. You should get a lot of rest, and drink plenty of water.
- Yes, sir. Thank you very much.
- Your welcome, feel better soon.

Chapter 10: Going to the Bank

Eu preciso pegar dinheiro

In this chapter we will discuss something that you definitely want to be well-informed on so that you don't make any major mistakes when dealing with your money. When you are traveling, studying, or working abroad you may choose to use a credit card, travelers cheques, an atm card, or to open your own bank account. Depending on where you go I Brazil you'll probably have to use cash for most transactions. In any of these cases, you will probably have to deal with going to the bank at least once during your stay, whether it be to transfer money home, withdraw, or exchange money. Below are some very useful phrases for you to deal with your money in a Portuguese-speaking country.

Banking Phrases

I need to withdraw money	Preciso pegar dinheiro.
deposit money	Depositar dinheiro
exchange money	Trocar dinheiro
How much is the dollar worth	Quanto está o dólar?
I want to open an account?	Quero abrir uma conta.
I want to transfer money.	Quero transferir dinheiro.
Cash	Em dinheiro
Currency	Moeda

Vocabulário – No banco

Credit Card	Cartão de crédito
Traveler's cheques	Cheques de viagem
Account	A conta
Cashier	Caixa
ATM	Caixa Automático
Loan	Empréstimo
Identification (ID)	Identificação (ID)
Amount	Quantidade

Exercícios!

Match the Vocabulary

1. caixa ----------------------------------a. loan
2. cheques de viagem-----------------------b. credit card
3. a conta--------------------------------c. amount
4. o empréstimo ---------------------------d. cashier
5. caixa automático----------------------e. currency
6. cartão de crédito----------------------f. ATM
7. quantidade--------------------------------g. cash
8. fazer câmbio-------------------------------h. to exchange
9. moeda------------------------------ i. traveler's cheques
10. dinheiro------------------------------j. account

Translate to English

- Boa tarde, como posso ajudá-lo?

- Olá, preciso trocar dinheiro.

- Ok.

- Quanto está o dólar?

- Um dólar está 2,50 reais.

- Ok, quero trocar cem dólares.

- Aquí está 250 reais.

-Obrigado.

-De nada. Tenha um bom dia.

Chapter 10 Answers

Match the Vocabulary

1. caixa -------------------------d. cashier
2. cheques de viagem ------------i. traveler's cheques
3. a conta----------------------j. account
4. o empréstimo ------------------a. loan
5. caixa automático-----------f. ATM
6. cartão de crédito------------b. credit card
7. quantidade-----------------------c. amount
8. fazer câmbio------------------------h. to exchange
9. moeda------------------------e. currency
10. dinheiro----------------------g. cash

Translation

- Boa tarde, como posso ajudá-lo?
- Olá, preciso trocar dinheiro.
- Ok.
- Quanto está o dólar?
- Um dólar está 2,50 reais.
- Ok, quero trocar cem dólares.
- Aquí está 250 reais.
-Obrigado.
-De nada. Tenha um bom dia.

- Hello, how can I help you?
- Hi, I need to exchange money.
- Okay.
- How much is the dollar worth?
- The dollar is worth 2.50 reais.
- Okay, I want to exchange 100 dollars.
- Here is 250 reais.
-Thank you very much.
- Your welcome, have a nice day.

Chapter 11: Transportation

Onde vamos?

Part 1: At the airport

This chapter will be divided into two sections: *At the Airport* and *Travelling by taxi, bus or train.* This section is dedicated to that ever exciting moment of arriving at the airport in the new country where you will study, play, sightsee, work or whatever your motive may be. In Brazil not even airport employees speak English, and even if they do it will be very limited English so it is always helpful if you are one step ahead and know how to say a few useful things to get you through customs, outside the airport, and ready to embark on your new adventure. Bon voyage or as they say in Portuguese: Boa viagem!

At the Airport

Airport	o Aeroporto
Airplane	O avião
Airline	A companhia aérea
Suitcase	A mala
Passport	o passaporte
Flight	o vôo
Customs	a alfândega
Ticket	A passagem
Baggage Claim Area	Área de retirada de bagagens
Gate	Portão
Terminal	O terminal
Destination	O destino
Have a good trip!	Boa viagem!

Useful Phrases at the Airport

When does the flight leave?	Quando sai o vôo?
When does the flight arrive?	Quando chega o vôo?
I have two suitcases.	Tenho duas malas
Where is terminal B?	Onde fica o terminal B?
I´m looking for gate 17.	Estou procurando o portão 17.
Where is the baggage claim?	Onde fica a área de retirada de

| | bagagens? |
| My suitcases are lost. | Minhas malas foram extraviadas. |

Exercícios!

Fill in the blank with the word from the word bank

O vôo ----- malas
O portão -----   a passagem
a companhia aérea ----- área de retirada de bagagens

1. Estou procurando _____ vinte e três.

2. Quando sai _____?

3. Minhas malas estão na _____.

4. Vou para a Espanha com a_____ AirFrance.

5. Tenho muitas _____ que estão na área de retirada de bagagens.

Match the Vocabulary

6. a alfândega --------------------a. Airplane

7. o destino---------------------b. Customs

8. a passagem----------------------c. Have a good trip

9. o avião----------------------d. Ticket

10. Boa viagem-------------------e. Destination

Translate to English

- Olá senhora, em que posso ajudar?

- Olá, quando é o vôo para Buenos Aires?

- Ele sai às quinze horas.

- O embarque é por que portão?

- Portão dez.

- OK, muito obrogada senhor.

- De nada, boa viagem!

Part 2: Travelling by taxi, bus, or train.

This section is dedicated to that travelling you will do within the city or from city to city in your new country. Knowing how to read the signs and ask around inside of the various bus and train stations will hopefully help you avoid getting completely lost. And if you do, it will help you to get out of the situation. I always suggest being flexible and ready for adventure because sometimes getting lost just means you get to experience a completely new scenery you´ve never seen before. Within the city, you may travel by bus, or taxi. Travelling by taxi is usually an excellent way to get language practice as you have your own personal conversation partner until you arrive to your destination. Also, if you're planning on going somewhere by taxi, either use your smartphone to check that the way they are going in the right one, or check the way in advance and ask the taxi driver to take the streets you want, and then check that they are doing that. Brazilians do that too! You will most likely travel by bus or plane to go from city to city. Happy exploring in your new country!

Taxi Vocabulary

Where are we going?	Para onde vamos?
I'm going to…	Vou para …
At the stoplight, turn right/left	No sinal/semáforo, vire à direita/esquerda
You can stop here.	Pode parar aqui.
Here on the right/left	Aqui à direita/esquerda
How much do I owe you?	Quanto te devo?

*As I mentioned in the intro, verbs in Portuguese have more changes according to their subject. These are called **conjugations**.

* Below is the conjugation of the verb: *Ir- to go*

Ir- to go

Eu -------**Vou** ------- **I go**

Tu/você -------- **Vais/vai** -------**you go**

ele, ela, ------- **Vai**-------**he, she goes**

nós-------**Vamos** --------**we go**

eles, elas, vocês ------- **Vão** -------**they**

Exercícios!

Put the verb *ir* in the correct form.

1. Eu _____ para São Paulo amanhã.

2. Onde nós_____ ?

3. Você _____ ao supermercado hoje?

4. Onde ela _____ ?

5. Eles _____ para o restaurante?

Match the Phrases

6. Vire à esquerda no sinal.------------------------a. Here on the right.

7. Onde vamos?----------------------b. How much do I owe you?

8. Aqui à direita----------------------c. You can stop here

9. Pode parar aqui---------------------d. Where are we going?

10. Quanto te devo? --------------------e. Turn left at the stoplight.

Bus and Train Vocabulary

The bus/train station	A estação de ônibus/trem
Bus stop	O ponto de ônibus
When does the next train leave for…?	Que horas sai o próximo trem para…?
Departures	Partidas
arrivals	Chegadas
I would like a one way ticket	Quero uma passagem só de ida.
Round trip ticket	Passagem de ida e volta
Which platform does the train leave from?	De qual plataforma o trem sai?
Do I need to change bus?	Preciso trocar de ônibus?
To get on…	embarcar
To get off..	descer

*Verb Conjugation

Sair- To leave
Eu-----------Saio - -----------I leave
Tu/você --------------------------Sais/sai ----------you leave
ele, ela -----------------Sai -----------he, she leaves
nós--------Saímos ------we leave
eles, elas, vocês -----------Saem ---------they leave

*Notice for *it leaves* you use the third conjugation, *sai.*

Ex: O trem **sai** às 7 =The train **leaves** at 7

O ônibus **sai** às 3:30 =The bus **leaves** at 3:30.

Exercícios!

Put the verb *sair* in the correct form.

11. Eu _____ para ir ao aeroporto às sete.

12. Que horas _____ o trem para Barcelona?

13. Você _____ para a aula às seis?

14. Que horas _____ o ônibus para Santiago?

15. Que horas eles _____ para o Rio?

Translate to English

- Bom dia, Em que posso ajudá-lo?

- Que horas sai o próximo ônibus para Búzios?

- Às oito da manhã.

- Obrigado. Quero uma passagem de ida e volta para Búzios.

- Ok.

- De qual plataforma sai o ônibus?

- Da plataforma treze.

- Ok, obrigado.

- De nada, boa viagem.

Chapter 11: Part 1 Answers

Fill in the blank with the word from the word bank

1. Estou procurando <u>o portão</u> vinte e três.

2. Quando sai <u>o vôo</u>?

3. Minhas malas estão na <u>área de retirada de bagagens</u>.

4. Vou para a Espanha com a <u>companhia aérea</u> AirFrance.

5. Tenho muitas <u>malas</u> que estão na área de retirada de bagagens.

Match the Vocabulary

6. a alfândega -------------b. Customs
7. o destino--------------e. Destination
9. o avião ---------------a. Airplane
10. Boa viagem------------c. Have a good trip.

Translation

- Olá senhora, em que posso ajudar?
- Olá, quando é o vôo para Buenos Aires?
- Ele sai às quinze horas.
- O embarque é por que portão?
- Portão dez.
- OK, muito obrigada senhor.
- De nada, boa viagem!

- Hi, ma'am, how can I help you?
- Hi, when does the flight to Buenos Aires leave?
- It takes off at 3:00 pm.
- What gate does it leave from?
- From gate 10.
- Okay, thank you sir.
- Your welcome, bon voyage!

Chapter 11: Part 2 Answers

Put the verb *ir* in the correct form

1. Eu vou para São Paulo amanhã.

2. Onde nós vamos ?

3. Você vai ao supermercado hoje?

4. Onde ela vai ?

5. Eles vão para o restaurante?

Match the Phrases

6. Vire à esquerda no sinal----- e. At the stoplight, turn left.

7. Onde vamos?----------------------------d. Where are we going?

8. Aqui à direita.---------------------------a. Here on the right

9. Pode parar aqui.---------------------------c. You can stop here.

10. Quanto te devo?---------------------------b. How much do I owe you?

Put the verb *sair* in the correct form

11. Eu saio para ir ao aeroporto às sete.

12. Que horas sai o trem para Barcelona?

13. Você sai para a aula às seis?

14. Que horas sai o ônibus para Santiago?

15. Que horas eles saem para o Rio?

Translation

- Bom dia, Em que posso ajudá-lo?

- Que horas sai o próximo ônibus para Búzios?
- Às oito da manhã.
- Obrigado. Quero uma passagem de ida e volta para Búzios.
- Ok.
- De qual plataforma sai o ônibus?
- Da plataforma treze.
- Ok, obrigado.
- De nada, boa viagem.

- Good morning, how can I help you?
- What time does the next bus leave for Búzios?
- It leaves at 8 in the morning.
- Thank you. I would like a round trip ticket to Búzios.
- Okay.
- Which platform does the bus leave from?
- From platform 13.
- Okay, thank you very much.
- Your welcome, have a good trip.

Chapter 12: Finding a place to stay

Quero reservar um quarto

Now that we have, hopefully, gotten you to your destination safe and sound, it is time to look for a place to stay. Whether you decide to stay in a hotel, hostel, or bed and breakfast, this chapter should help you through every step of the way. Remember that some of the luxuries we are used to like *água quente* (hot water) cannot always be expected. Below, I have listed useful vocabulary and phrases for booking a room at your new destination. Enjoy your stay!

Hotel Vocabulary

I would like to reserve a room for one/two people.	Eu gostaria de reservar um quarto para um/dois
How much does it cost per day?	Quanto custa a diária?
For how many people?	Para quantas pessoas?
For how many days?	Quantas diárias?
Para una noche/dos noches	Uma diária/duas diárias
With a double bed.	Com cama de casal.
With two single beds	Com duas camas de solteiro
I'm sorry, we are full.	Sinto muito, estamos lotados.
I have a reservation.	Tenho uma reserva.
Do you have wi-fi?	Tem wi-fi?

Exercícios!

Match the Phrases

1. I'm sorry we are full------------------------a. Tenho uma reserva.

2. For how many people?---------------------b. Quantas diárias?

3. I have a reservation.------------------------c. Quanto custa a diária?

4. For how many days?-----------------------d. Sinto muito, estamos lotados.

5. How much is it per day?-------------------e. Para quantas pessoas?

Translate to English

- Boa noite.

- Boa noite, como posso ajudar?

- Eu gostaria de reservar um quarto para um.

- Por quantos dias?

- Para três dias.

- Ok.

- Quanto é a diária?

- Cem reais por noite.

- Aqui tem wi-fi?

- Sim, temos wi-fi.

- Obrigado, senhor.

Chapter 12 Answers

Match the Phrases

1. I'm sorry we are full-----------------d. Sinto muito, estamos lotados.
2. For how many people?-------------e. Para quantas pessoas?
3. I have a reservation.----------------a. Eu tenho uma reserva.
4. For how many days?--------------b. Para quantos dias?
5. How much is it per day?----------c. Quanto custa a diária?

Translation

- Boa noite.
- Boa noite, como posso ajudar?
- Eu gostaria de reservar um quarto para um.
- Por quantos dias?
- Para três dias.
- Ok.
- Quanto é a diária?
- Cem reais por noite.
- Aqui tem wi-fi?
- Sim, temos wi-fi.
- Obrigado, senhor.

- Good evening.
- Good evening, ma'am, how can I help you?
- I would like to reserve a room for one person.
- For how many nights?
-- For three nights
- Okay.
- How much is it per night?
- 100 dollars per night.
- And do you have wi-fi?
- Yes, we have wi-fi.
- Thank you, sir.

SECTION 3: GETTING TO KNOW EACH OTHER

Chapter 13: Description

Como é?

Now that we have gotten you through the essentials of getting around, finding a place to stay, and all of the other basics, we can focus on having a conversation in order to get to know people, make friends, etc. By the end of this section you will be able to talk about yourself, your family, work, and hobbies. The first chapter of this section is focused on description- how to describe yourself, other people, and things to others. Below, I have listed some useful vocabulary and phrases to help you describe the world around you.

Description Vocabulary

tall	alto/a
short	baixo/a
fat	gordo/a
thin	magro/a
pretty	bonito/a
cute	lindo/a
hair	cabelo
short (length)	curto/a
long	longo/a
big	grande
small	pequeno/a
strong	forte
ugly	feio/a
old	velho/a
young	jovem

*Why can most of the Portuguese adjectives end in **o** or **a** like *lindo* or *linda*?

*Quick review- Which is correct, garoto linda or garoto lindo?

*If you said garot**o** lind**o**, you are right!
Don't forget to match the adjective to gender and number of the noun.

Description Phrases and More Vocabulary

What's it like?	Como é?

What does he/she look like?	Como é ele/ela?
He is…/She is …	ele é …/Ela é …
I am…	Eu sou …
What color is his/her hair?	Qual é a cor do seu cabelo?
His/her hair is….	O cabelo dele/dela é ….
Does she have long hair?	Ela tem cabelo longo?
He has short hair.	Ele tem cabelo curto.
blonde	loiro/a
brunette	moreno/a
red headed	ruivo/a

*Verb Conjugation

Ser- to be (permanent)

Eu-------------**Sou**------------I am

Tu/você------------**és/é**-----------you are

ele, ela----**é**-------------he, she is

nós-----**Somos**----we are

eles, elas, vocês-----**São**--------they are

Exercícios!

Put the verb *ser* in the correct form and translate the sentence.

1. Eu_____ muito alta e magra--
_____

2. Ela _____ baixa e linda.------
_____

3. Ele _____ muito velho?----------
_____

4. Nós _____ bonitos.-------
_____

5. Eles _____ fortes. -------------
_____

Translate the Phrases

1. Como ela é? --------------------------

_____

2. Ela é alta, jovem, e bonita.------------

_____

3. De que cor é o seu cabelo?--------------

_____

4. Ela tem cabelo ruivo e longo.--------

_____

5. Ele tem cabelo curto?------------------

_____

6. Sim, ele tem cabelo curto e preto.---------

_____

*Below I will list some words to describe your emotions. You should use forms of the verb *estar* to talk about your emotions.

Ex: estou feliz.=I am happy.

Emotion Vocabulary

How do you feel?	Como você está se sentindo?
I feel…	estou…
Happy	Feliz, contente/a
Sad	Triste
Tired	Cansado/a
Excited	Empolgado/a
Bored	Entediado/a
Angry	Zangado/a
Nervous	Nervoso/a
Calm	Tranquilo/a
Busy	Ocupado/a
Scared	Assustado/a

*Verb Conjugation

Estar- to be (Temporary)

Eu----Estou-----I am

Tu/você------**Estás/está**-------**you are**

ele, ela------**Está**-------**he, she is**

nós-----**Estamos**-----**we are**

eles, elas, vocês------ **Estão**------**they, you**

Match the Vocabulary

1. happy--a. entediado
2. excited--b. ocupada
3. nervous---c. cansada
4. bored--d. assustado
5. angry--e. Zangado
6. sad --f. tranquila
7. calm--g. feliz
8. busy--h. empolgado
9. scared---i. triste
10. tired--j. nervosa

Put the verb *estar* in the correct form and translate the sentence.

1. Eu _____ muito triste._____

2. Ela _____ contente hoje._____

3. Ele _____ nervoso?_____

4. Nós _____ tranquilos._____

5. Elas _____ assustadas.
_____

Chapter 13 Answers

Put the verb *ser* in the correct form and translate the sentence.

1. Eu sou muito alta e magra. ------ I am very tall and thin.

2. Ela é baixa e linda. --------------She is short and cute.

3. Ele é muito velho?----------------- Is he very old?

4. Nós somos muito bonitos. -------We are very handsome.

5. Eles são fortes. ------------------They are strong.

Translate the Phrases

1. Como ela é? ---------------------------What is she like?

2. Ela é alta, jovem, e bonita.-------------She is tall, young, and pretty.

3. De que cor é o seu cabelo?----------------What color is his/her hair?

4. Ela tem cabelo ruivo e longo.--------She has long and blonde hair.

5. Ele tem cabelo curto? ------------------Does he have short hair?

6. Sim, ele tem cabelo curto e preto----------Yes, he has short, black hair.

Match the Vocabulary

1. happy ------------g. feliz
2. Excited-----------h. empolgado
3. Nervous----------j. nervosa
4. bored ------------a. entediado
5. Angry-------------e. zangado
6. Sad----------------i. triste
7. Calm--------------f. tranquila
8. Busy-------------b. ocupada
9. Scared-----------d. assustado
10. Tired-----------c. cansada

Put the verb *estar* in the correct form and translate the sentence.

1. Eu estou muito triste.----------------I am very sad.
2. Ela está contente hoje. -----------She is happy today.
3. Ele está nervoso?------------------Is he nervous?
4. Nós estamos tranquilos.-----We are calm.
5. Elas estão assustadas.---------------They are scared.

Chapter 14: We are family

Quantos irmãos você tem?

In this chapter you will be able to talk about your family – how many brothers and sisters you have, whether they are older or younger, etc. You will also be able to talk about your extended family- aunts, uncles, cousins, grandparents, etc. When you travel to a Portuguese-speaking country, you will realize the importance that family plays in an individual's life. Families are very close and place emphasis on taking care of one another. We will also learn the conjugation of a very useful verb *ter* so you can discuss what you and others have. Below you will learn useful language to describe your family.

Family vocabulary and phrases

How many siblings do you have?	Quantos irmãos você tem?
I have 3 siblings.	Tenho 3 irmãos.
Brother	Irmão
Sister	Irmã
Mom	Mamãe
Dad	Papai
Mother	Mãe
Father	Pai
grandpa/grandma	avô/avó
cousin (female/male)	primo/prima
husband/wife	esposo/esposa
son/daughter	filho/filha
uncle/aunt	tio/tia
Pet	Bicho de estimação
Dog	Cachorro
Cat	Gato
Older	Mais velho
Younger	Mais novo

* Remember that the adjective comes after the noun.
younger brother = irmão mais novo
older sister = irmã mais velha

*Verb Conjugation

Ter- to have
Eu ----------------------Tenho -------------I have
Tu/você-----------------------Tens/tem-------------you have
ele, ela-------------Tem -------------he, she has
nós---Temos --------we have
eles, elas, vocês-------Têm------------they, you have

*It's useful to know the possessive pronouns in order to talk about family, so you can say – *my* mom, *his* sister, *her* grandma, etc.

Possessive Pronouns

My	Meu/Minha – meus/minhas
Your	seu/sua – seus/suas
His or Her	dele/dela
Our	Nosso/Nossa/Nossos/Nossas
Their	deles/delas

*Notice you have to match it with the number of what is yours and for nosso the number and the gender.
Ex: My brother = Meu irmão
My siblings = Meus irmãos
Our grandma = Nossa avó

Exercícios!

Put the verb *ter* in the correct form and translate the sentence.

1. Eu_____três irmãos.
_____
2. Ele _____ dez primos.
_____
3. Ela _____ muitos irmãos?
_____
4. Nós _____ dois filhos.
_____
5. Eles _____ um cachorro e um gato.
_____

Match the Vocabulary

1. esposo —— a. grandma

2. esposa —— b. pet

3. tio —— c. older

4. tia —— d. aunt

5. mais velho —— e. dad

6. mais novo —— f. grandpa

7. bicho de estimação —— g. husband

8. avô —— h. wife

9. avó —— i. younger

10. papai —— j. uncle

Put the possessive pronoun in the correct form

1. (My) _____ irmão são muito altos.

2. (His) A irmã _____ é bonita.

3. (Our) _____ avó é muito simpática.

4. (Your) _____ pais são baixos?

5. (Their) Os avôs deles são muito velhos?

Write about your family following the example

Eu tenho um irmão mais velho. Ele tem 33 anos e se chama Jacob. Ele tem uma esposa chamada Annie. O nome da minha mãe é Ruth e meu pai se chama Keith. Tenho doze primos no total. Três primos, nove primas. Também tenho um marido e um filho. Alberto e Elias. Eu tenho duas avós que vivem no Texas e uma avó que mora em Oklahoma.

Chapter 14 Answers

Put the verb *tener* in the correct form and translate the sentence.

1. Eu <u>tenho</u> três irmãos. ---------------<u>I have three brothers.</u>
2. Ele <u>tem</u> dez primos. -------------------<u>He has ten cousins.</u>
3. Ela <u>tem</u> muitos irmãos?------<u>Does she have many siblings?</u>
4. Nós <u>temos</u> dois filhos.---------<u>We have two children.</u>
5. Eles <u>têm</u> um cachorro e um gato. -------<u>They have a dog and a cat.</u>

Match the Vocabulary

1. esposo ---------g. husband
2. esposa ----------h. wife
3. tio --------------j. uncle
4. tio --------------d. aunt
5. mais velho----------c. older
6. mais novo----------i. younger
7. bicho de estimação-------b. husband
8. avô---------f. grandpa
9. avó----------a. grandma
10. papai ----------e. dad

Put the possessive pronoun in the correct form

1. (My) <u>Meu</u> irmão são muito altos.

2. (His) A irmã <u>dele</u> é bonita.

3. (Our) <u>Nossa</u> avó é muito simpática.

4. (Your) <u>Seus</u> pais são baixos?

5. (Their) Os avôs <u>deles</u> são muito velhos?

Write about your family following the example

Various possible answers.

Chapter 15: All work and no play

Com que você trabalha?

Now that we are able to describe ourselves physically and discuss our family, we can talk about what we do, our career. It is something that we often talk about and sometimes can, unfortunately, consume our lives. In Brazil you'll see that they are often surprised at how work is such a big part of our lives. As I mentioned in the previous chapter, helping each other out as friends and family is often more important than one's individual career and success. In this chapter, you will learn some basic professions of our society.

Occupational vocabulary and phrases

What do you do?	Com o que você trabalha?/ O que você faz?
I am a teacher.	Sou professora.
teacher	professor/professora
businessman/business woman	empresário/empresária
Doctor	mádico/médica
Nurse	enfermeiro/enfermeira
Lawyer	advogado/advogada
Writer	escritor/escritora
policeman	Polical
firefighter	bombeiro/bombeira
student	estudante
receptionist	recepcionista
Waiter	garçom/garçonete
Cook	cozinheiro/cozinheira
salesperson	vendedor/vendedora
engineer	engenheiro/engenheira

*By now, you can probably guess why most of the occupations end in either *o* or *a*

Ex: advogado = lawyer (male)

Advogada = lawyer (female)

*Portuguese differentiates between females and males much more often in its words. You notice when you say lawyer in English, we don't know whether the person is a he or she, in Portuguese, you immediately know.

Exercícios!

Match the Vocabulary

1. advogada-----------------------------------a. police officer

2. bombeiro-----------------------------------b. nurse

3. garçom--------------------------------------c. doctor

4. cozinheira ---------------------------------d. businessman

5. engenheira---------------------------------e. salesperson

6. enfermeiro---------------------------------f. waiter

7. empresário--------------------------------g. firefighter

8. vendedor----------------------------------h. attorney

9. médica--------------------------------------i. engineer

10. policial-----------------------------------j. cook

Put the correct form of the word according to gender.

1. Ela é _____ (advogado/advogada).

2. Eles são _____ (bombeiros/bombeiro).

3. Ele é _____ (professor/professora).

4. Elas são _____ (escritores/escritoras).

5. Eu sou _____ (empresário/ empresária). (Answer according to your gender)

Answer the following question about your occupation. Don't forget to answer according to your gender.

Com o que você trabalha?
_____

Chapter 15 Answers

Match the Vocabulary

1. advogada ------h. attorney
2. bombeiro------g. firefighter
3. garçom--------f. waiter
4. cozinheira ------j. cook
5. engenheira-----i. engineer
6. enfermeiro----b. nurse
7. empresário----d. businessman
8. vendedor-----e. salesperson
9. médica-------c. doctor
10. policial------a. police officer

Put the correct form of the word according to gender.

1. Ela é advogada (advogado/advogada).

2. Eles são bombeiros (bombeiros/bombeiro).

3. Ele é professor (professor/professora).

4. Elas são escritoras (escritores/escritoras).

5. Sou answers will vary (empresário/ empresária). (Answer according to your gender)

Com que você trabalha.?

Answers will vary.

Chapter 16: Hobbies

O que você gosta de fazer?

Now that we have learned how to describe yourself, your family, and occupation, we can move on to discussing what you enjoy doing in your free time. Once again, a cultural difference that you will see in Brazil is that they often spend their free time with family, a great contrast to our culture. Below you will find useful phrases to discuss our hobbies and also an explanation of the verb *gostar* so that you can talk about what you like.

Vocabulary to discuss your Hobbies

What do you like to do?	O que você gosta de fazer?
I like …	Eu gusto de…
I don't like	Não gusto de…
free time	tempo livre
play sports	Fazer esportes
play videogames	jogar videogames
travel	viajar
read	ler
go to the movies	ir ao cinema
go to the beach	ir à praia
watch TV	assistir televisão
watch sports	assistir esportes
listen to music	escutar música
play an instrument	tocar um instrumento
ski	esquiar
spend time with friends	passar tempo com amigos

*Notice that most of the verbs in Portuguese end in *ar, er, ir*. These are called infinitives.

Ex: jogar = to play

*You will learn how to conjugate regular verbs in the last section of this book.

Exercícios!

Choose the correct answer

1. I like to go to the movies.

a. Ele gosta de ir à praia.--------------b. Eu gosto de ir ao cinema.

c. Você gosta de ir ao cinema?.----------------d. Nós gostamos de ir ao cinema.

2. Do you like to read?

a. Você gosta de ler? --------------------b. Nós gostamos de ler?

c. Eles gostam de tocar guitarra? .-------------------d. Você gosta de andar?

3. I don't like to travel.
a. Eu não gosto de viajar-------------- b. Eu não gosto de jogar.
c. Ele não gosta de jogar------------------d. Você não gosta de viajar?

Match the Verb Phrases
1. Fazer esportes---------------------------------a. Spend time with friends
2. Ir à praia   ------------------------------------b. Play videogames
3. Passar tempo com amigos ------------------ c. Watch sports.
4. Assistir esportes ---------------------------------- d. Go to the beach
5. Jogar videogames-----------------------------e. Play sports

Chapter 16 Answers

Choose the correct answer

1. I like to go to the movies.

c. Eu gosto de ir ao cinema.

2. Do you like to read?

d. Você gosta de ler?

3. I don't like to travel.

d. Não gosto de viajar.

Match the Verb Phrases

1. fazer esportes   e. Play sports
2. Ir à praia   d. Go to the beach
3. Passar tempo com amigos   a. Spend time with friends
4. Assistir esportes   c. Watch sports.
5. Jogar videogames   b. Play videogames

SECTION 4: GRAMMAR SCHOOL

Some of the Most Challenging Grammar Topics for Portuguese Learners

Chapter 17: To be or not to be

Ser e Estar

In the last section of this crash course we will discuss some of the difficult grammar topics of Portuguese in the simplest way possible. As I have said, languages cannot be translated word for word and often one word in one language can be communicated in more than one way depending on the situation. One of these words in English is *to be* which in Portuguese can be said in two ways *ser* or *estar* depending on the specific circumstances. We find this difficult because we must think harder about what is being or not being. Below I will explain when to use each and we will review how to conjugate these verbs.

Ser- to be (Generally for permanent states)

Rule	English Example	Portuguese Example
Origin	I am from Spain.	Sou da Espanha.
Description	Her car is red.	Seu carro é vermelho.
Occupation	I am a nurse.	Eu sou enfermeira.
Date	Today is January 4th.	Hoje é dia 4 de janeiro.
Time	It is 3:00.	São 15h
Characteristic	She is tall.	Ela é alta
Permanent position	My house is on 5 street	Minha casa é na rua 5

Estar-to be (Generally used for temporary conditions)

Rule	English Example	Portuguese Example
Temporary Position	The cup is on the table	O copo está na mesa
Action	He is travelling to Chile.	Ele está viajando para o Chile.
Condition	Are you sick?	Você está doente?
Emotion	I'm bored.	Estou entediado.

*Let's look at some differences between *ser* and *estar*

Ser is used to talk about the general characteristic of something.

Estar is used to talk about the condition of something.

Ex: Bananas are yellow. = Bananas são amarelas. *(In general bananas are yellow)*
This banana is green. = Esta banana está verde *(This specific banana is green now and it could change once it matures)*

Peixe é delicioso.= Fish is delicious *(Generally speaking, fish is delicious)*
Este peixe está delicioso =   This fish is delicious.
(This fish I am eating now is delicious)
*Do you get the general idea now?
- *ser* describes the general charactistic of things.
- *estar* describes the specific state of things in this moment.

Exercícios!

See if you can remember how to conjugate the verbs *Ser* and *Estar* below

Ser- to be (permanent)
Eu _____
Tu/você _____
ele, ela _____
nós _____
eles, elas, vocês_____

Estar- to be (temporary)
eu_____
tu/você_____
ele, ela_____
nós_____
eles, elas,vocês _____

Fill in the blank with the correct form of *ser* or *estar*
1. Eu _____ (sou/estou) dos Estados Unidos.
2. O cachorro _____ (é/está) preto.
3. Ele _____ (é/está) muito contente.
4. Elas _____ (são/estão) professores.
5. O correio _____ (é/está) ao lado do supermercado.
6. Nós _____ (somos/estamos) falando espanhol.
7. Eu _____ (sou/estou) muito alta.
8. _____ (são/estão) cinco da tarde.
9. Você _____ (é/está) doente?

10. Hoje _____ (é/está) dia cinco de maio.

Chapter 17 Answers

See if you can remember how to conjugate the verbs *Ser* and *Estar* below

Ser- to be (permanent)

Eu ------ Sou
Tu/você------ é<u>s</u>/<u>é</u>
ele, ela,-------- é
nós ------ <u>Somos</u>
eles, elas, vocês--------- são

Estar- to be (temporary)

Eu ------- Estou
Tu/você ------ <u>Estás/está</u>
ele, ela ------<u>Está</u>
nós -----<u>Estamos</u>
eles, elas, vocês -----<u>Estão</u>

Fill in the blank with the correct form of *ser* or *estar*

1. Eu <u>sou</u> (sou/estou) dos Estados Unidos.

2. O cachorro <u>é</u> (é/está) preto.

3. Ele <u>está</u> (é/está) muito contente.

4. Elas <u>são</u> (são/estão) professoras.

5. O correio <u>é</u> (é/está) ao lado do supermercado.

6. Nós <u>estamos</u> (somos/estamos) falando espanhol.

7. Eu <u>sou</u> (sou/estou) muito alta.

8. <u>São</u> (são/estão) cinco da tarde.

9. Você <u>está</u> (é/está) doente?

10. Hoje é (é/está) dia cinco de maio.

Chapter 18: Por e para

In this chapter we will discuss the differences between *por* and *para.* They can both usually be translated as *for* and for this reason can be quite confusing to non-native speakers of Portuguese. I will clear up this confusion and explain when to use each below.

Por- Generally used to express movement through time or space

Rule	English Example	Portuguese Example
To show thanks	Thank you for your help	Obrigado por sua ajuda.
Per (time period)	How much is it per night?	Quanto é por noite?
To show length of time	I studied for 5 hours.	Estudei por 5 horas.
To show means of communication	We talk on Skype.	Conversamos por Skype.

Para – Generally used to show destination for something.

Rule	English Example	Portuguese Example
Showing your destination (place)	The bus leaves for Búzios at 4 pm	O ônibus sai para Búzios às 16h.
Showing for whom something is	The surprise is for Lorena.	A surpresa é para a Lorena.
Showing when something is due	The homework is due Monday.	O dever de casa é para segunda.
To show a goal for something	I study a lot in order to achieve what I want.	Estudo muito para conseguir o que quero.

Other common and useful phrases with por and para

- por exemplo ----- for example
- por isso ----------- that's why
- por fim------------- finally
- por favor ----------please
- por aqui -----------around here

-
- para que-------- so that
- Para que? --------why? for what purpose?
- para sempre-----------forever

105

Exercícios!

Put *por* or *para* in the blank.

1. Vou _____ aula amanhã.

2. Tenho uma surpresa _____ minha mamãe.

3. O ônibus sai _____ San Juan às duas.

4. Quando sai o trem _____ a capital?

5. O dever de casa é _____ quinta.

6. _____ que você não vai de avião?

7. A conta _____ favor.

9. Vou _____ um vestido novo.

10. Estudo muito _____ entrar para a universidade.

Chapter 18 Answers

Put *por* or *para* in the blank.

1. Vou para aula amanhã.

2. Tenho uma surpresa para minha mamãe.

3. O ônibus sai para San Juan às duas.

4. Quando sai o trem para a capital?

5. O dever de casa é para quinta.

6. Por que você não vai de avião?

7. A conta por favor.

9. Vou por um vestido novo.

10. Estudo muito para entrar para a universidade.

Chapter 19: Conjugating Regular Verbs in the Present

Another confusing aspect of Portuguese is the need for so many verb changes. In English, we usually have two changes in the present. For example, *I walk,* you *walk,* he or she *walks,* we *walk,* etc. It only changes in the *he* or *she* form from *walk* to *walks*. In Portuguese, you would have five changes for this verb. Regular verbs are divided into three kinds: verbs that end in *ar, er,* or *ir* verbs. We have already conjugated throughout this book several irregular and commonly used verbs. Below, we will discuss conjugating mostly regular verbs in the present and a few more common irregular verbs.

Steps for Conjugating Regular Present Verbs:

1. Remove the ending: *ar, er,* or *ir*

2. Identify what the subject is: *I, you, he, she, we,* etc.

3. Attach the corresponding ending to the verb.

'ar' verbs

Fal*ar*- to talk > remove the *ar* > *fal* > attach the correct ending

Eu	O	Fal**o**	=	I talk
Tu/você	As/a	fal**as**/fal**a**	=	you talk
Ele, ela	A	Fal**a**	=	he, she talks; you talk
Nós	Amos	Fal**amos**	=	we talk
Eles, elas, vocês	am	Fal**am**	=	they, you all talk

*Let's say you want to say *we walk:*

And*ar*- to walk > remove the *ar* > *and* >

attach the correct ending- *amos* = andamos- we walk

108

'er' verbs

Comer- to eat > remove the *er* > *com* > attach the correct ending

Eu	O	com**o**	=	I eat
Tu/você	es/e	com**es**/com**e**	=	you eat
Ele,ela	E	com**e**	=	he, she eats; you eat
Nós	emos	com**emos**	=	we eat
Eles, elas, vocês	em	com**em**	=	they, you all talk

*Note- *ir* verbs have the same ending as *er*, except for *nós:*

'ir' verbs

Abrir- to open > remove the *ir* > *abr* > attach the correct ending

Eu	O	Abr**o**	=	I eat
Tu/você	es/e	abr**es**/abr**e**	=	you eat
Ele,ela	E	abr**e**	=	he, she eats; you eat
Nós	imos	abr**imos**	=	we eat
Eles, elas, vocês	em	abr**em**	=	they, you all talk

Exercícios!

Put the verbs in the correct form and translate the sentences.

1. Ele _____ (viajar) para o Chile amanhã._____

2. Eu _____ (comer)muita salada.
_____

3. Você _____ (beber) muito?
_____

4. Ela _____ (morar) em Nova York?
_____

5. Vocês _____ (falar) português?
_____

6. Nós _____ (acampar) nos Andes.
_____

7. Ela _____ (escutar) rock?
_____

8. Eles _____ (tocar) instrumentos.
_____

9. Eu _____ (passar) tempo com amigos._____

10. Eu _____ (abrir) a porta para os outros?
_____

* Common Irregular Verb Conjugations

Throughout the previous chapters we have already conjugated the following common irregular verbs: *estar, ser, ter, gostar,* and *ir*. In this chapter we will add five more of the most used verbs in the Portuguese language: *poder, querer, saber, dizer,* and f*azer.*

poder- to be able to
querer- to want
saber- to know
dizer- to say
fazer- to do/make

Poder- to be able to

Eu	**Posso**	-	I can
Tu/você	**Podes/Pode**	-	you can
Ele, ela	**Pode**	-	he, she can; you can
Nós	**Podemos**	-	we can
Eles, elas, vocês	**Podem**	-	they, you all can

*In order to say: I can do something, just add the *infinitive* after the form of *poder*.

Ex: I can ski = Eu posso esquiar
We can go today. = Nós podemos ir hoje.

Querer- to want

Eu	**Quero**	-	I want
Tu/você	**Queres/Quer**	-	you want
Ele,ela	**Quer**	-	he, she wants; you want
Nós	**Queremos**	-	we want
Eles, elas, vocês	**Querem**	-	they, you all want

Saber- to know

Eu	**Sei**	-	I know
Tu/você	**Sabes/Sabe**	-	you know
Ele,ela	**Sabe**	-	he, she knows; you know
Nós	**Sabemos**	-	we know
Eles, elas, vocês	**Sabem**	-	they, you all know

Fazer- to do/to make

Eu	**Faço**	-	I do
Tu/você	**Fazes /Faz**	-	you do
Ele,ela	**Faz**	-	he, she does; you do
Nós	**Fazemos**	-	we do
Eles, elas, vocês	**Fazem**	-	they, you all do

Dizer- to say

Eu	**Digo**	-	I say
Tu/você	**Dizes/Diz**	-	you say
Ele,ela	**Diz**	-	he, she says; you say
Nós	**Dizemos**	-	we say
Eles, elas, vocês	**Dizem**	-	they, you all say

* I am going to also conjugate *dizer* in the past tense because of how frequently it is used. Dizer in the past can mean- said, told, spoke

Dizer- to say (Past tense)

Eu	**Disse**	- I said
Tu/você	**Dissestes/disse**	- you can
Ele,ela	**Disse**	- he, she can; you can
Nós	**Dissemos**	- we can
Eles, elas, vocês	**Disseram**	- they, you all can

*Useful phrases with *dizer* - Some of the most frequently said things that I found very useful when I first lived in a Portuguese-speaking country.

(ele/ela) **me disse**	=	(he/she) **told me**
disse para ele	=	**I told** him/her/you
te disse	=	**I told you**
lhes disse	=	**I told** them/you all

Exercícios!

Put the verbs in the correct form.

1. Ela _____ (poder) falar inglês.
2. Eu _____ (saber) esquiar muito bem.
3. Você _____ (querer) ir para a praia?
4. Elas _____ (fazer) la tarea de matemáticas.
5. Nós _____ (saber) falar português.

Put the verbs in the correct form and translate the sentences.

6. Nós _____ (poder) ir ao cinema.
_____
7. O que você_____ (fazer) em seu tempo livre?_____
8. Eles _____ (querer) ir para a Argentina._____
9. Eu _____ (dizer- past) olá.
_____
10. Você_____ (poder) ver a televisão?
_____

Translate into Portuguese.

11. I told him _____

12. He told me _____

13. I told you _____

14. I told them _____

15. She told me _____

Chapter 19 Answers

1. Ele _____ (viajar) para o Chile amanhã._____
2. Eu _____ (comer) muita salada.
_____
3. Você _____ (beber) muito?
_____
4. Ela _____ (morar) em Nova York?
_____
5. Vocês _____ (falar)português?
_____
6. Nós _____(acampar) nos Andes.
_____
7. Ela _____(escutar) rock?
_____
8. Eles _____(tocar) instrumentos.
_____
9. Eu _____(passar) tempo com amigos._____
10. Eu _____(abrir) a porta para os outros.
_____

Put the verbs in the correct form and translate the sentences.

1. Ele <u>viaja</u> (viajar) para o Chile amanhã.　　He travels to Chile tomorrow.
2. Eu <u>como</u>(comer)muita salada.　　　　　　　I eat a lot of salad.
3. Você <u>bebe</u> muito?　　　　　　　　　　　　　Do you drink a lot?
4. Ela <u>mora</u> (morar) en Nueva York?　　　　　Does she live in New York?
5. Vocês <u>falam</u> (falar)português?　　　　　　Do you all speak Portuguese?
6. Nós <u>acampamos</u>(acampar) nos Andes.　　We ski in the Andes.
7. Elas <u>escutam</u> (escutar) rock?　　　　　　　Do you listen to rock music?
8. Eles <u>tocam</u> (tocar) instrumentos.　　　　　They play an instrument.
9. Eu <u>passo</u> (passar) tempo com amigos.　　I spend time with friends.
10. Eu <u>abro</u> (abrir) a porta para os outros.　I open the door for other people

Put the verbs in the correct form.

1. Ela <u>pode</u> (poder) **fa**lar inglés.
2. Eu <u>sei</u> (saber)esquiar muito bem.
3. Você <u>quer</u> (querer) ir à praia?

4. Elas <u>fazem</u> (fazer) o dever de matemática.
5. Vocês <u>sabem</u> (saber) falar português?

Put the verbs in the correct form and translate the sentences.

6. Nós <u>podemos</u> (poder) ir ao cinema.   <u>We can go to the movies.</u>
7. O que você <u>faz</u> (fazer) no seu tempo libre?   <u>What do you all do in your free time?</u>
8. Eles <u>querem</u> (querer) ir para a Argentina.   <u>They want to go to Argentina.</u>
9. Eu <u>disse</u> (dizer- past) olá.   <u>I said hi.</u>
10. Vocês <u>podem</u> (poder) ver a televisão?   <u>Can you all watch tv?</u>

Translate into Portuguese.

11. I told him   <u>Disse para ele</u>
12. He told me   <u>Ele me disse</u>
13. I told you   <u>Eu te disse</u>
14. I told them   <u>Lhes disse</u>
15. She told me   <u>Ela me disse</u>

Chapter 20: Ter ou não Ter

To be with hunger, to be with sleepiness, to be with thirst?

In this last chapter we will deal with the unusual way in which you express certain feelings or needs that you have. In English, we often use the verb- *to be*. *I am hot, you are cold, he is scared*, etc. Instead of saying, *I am hungry, I am thirsty, I am sleepy*; you say that *you are with* all of these feelings or conditions. This is not used with every adjective that expresses how you feel, so you must memorize in which situations *ter* should be used. Some of the situations in which you should use *ter* include when you are describing being sleepy, hungry, thirsty, scared, hot, cold, and even including when you are telling your age. *I have* thirty years, instead of *I am* thirty years old. It's a strange thing for us English speakers to comprehend but as I have said many times, NO language can be translated word for word. We have to remember to instead translate the ideas and keep in mind that in each language ideas are expressed in very different ways. Below, I have listed some 'ter and estar com expressions' with some questions for practice.

List of 'ter expressions'

ter ____ anos   -   to be ___ years old

estar com fome   -   to be hungry

estar com sede   -   to be thirsty

estar com frio   -   to be cold

estar com calor   -   to be hot

estar com sono   -   to be sleepy

estar com pressa -   to be in a hurry

ter medo   -   to be scared

ter cuidado   -   to be careful

tenha cuidado!   -   Be careful!

ter razão   -   to be right

ter sucesso   -   to be successful

ter ciúmes   -   to be jealous

ter sorte   -   to be lucky

ter vontade de   -   to feel like (doing something)

estar confiante   -   to be confident

estar com vergonha - to be embarrassed

Note: If you want to emphasize the feeling, I am very thirsty, sleepy, etc., in most cases you add 'muito' or 'muita' before the adjective.

Ex: Estou com **muita** fome   = I am **very** hungry
          Você está com **muito** sono = You are **very** sleepy
          Estamos com **muita** sede   = We are **very** thirsty

Exercícios!

Translate the expressions into English

1. Hoje estou com muito sono._____

2. Quantos anos você tem?_____

3. Tenho trinta anos. _____

4. Estamos com muito frio. _____

5. Você está com sede? Quer tomar água?_____

6. Estou com muito calor. Sim, quero tomar água._____

7. Tenho muito medo de crocodilos! _____

8. Tenha cuidado! Tem um cachorro muito grande._____

9. Meu amigo tem muita sorte. Ele ganhou 1.000 dólares! _____

10. Estou com vontade de comer pizza. _____

Tip: Remember to use context clues if you don't know a word. Making an educated guess based on the words is always helpful! It's one of the most important skills to have when learning a language.

Chapter 20 Answers

Translate the expressions into English

1. Hoje estou com muito sono.--------------<u>I am very sleepy today.</u>

2. Quantos anos você tem?   ----------------<u>How old are you?</u>

3. Tenho trinta anos. -------------------<u>I am thirty years old.</u>

4. Estamos com muito frio. -------------------<u>We are very cold.</u>

5. Você está com sede? Quer tomar água?------<u>Are you thirsty? Do you want to drink water?</u>

6. Estou com muito calor. Sim, quero tomar água.----------------<u>I am very hot. Yes, I want to drink water.</u>

7. Tenho muito medo de crocodilos! ------------<u>I am very scared of crocodiles.</u>

8. Tenha cuidado! Temu m cachorro muito grande. -------<u>Be careful! There is a very big dog.</u>

9. Meu amigo tem muita sorte. Ele ganhou 1.000 dólares!--------------<u>My friend is very lucky. He won 1,000 dollars.</u>

10. Estou com vontade de comer pizza. -------<u>I feel like eating pizza.</u>

Chapter 21: Portuguese Around the World

Ora pois, onde vais?

Portugal colonized a number of countries, Brazil was its "crown jewel" and at one point it even became the center of the Portuguese empire. The Portuguese language extends to the following countries too: East Timor, Mozambique, Angola, Cape Verde, São Tome and Principe, Guinea Bissau and Macau.

British and American English are the most comprehensive denominations of the English language, even though it is spoken on various other countries, and their equivalent for the Portuguese language is the comparison between Portuguese from Brazil and from Portugal.
In Brazil the language evolved influenced by a multitude of other languages, we had Spanish, African and English influences almost from the beginning. This made our Portuguese very characteristic, so much so that it wasn't until a few years ago, when we signed the Orthographic Agreement, that these two languages could be called variations of one language, instead of two separate ones.

Even though there are many other regional variations, the other Portuguese speaking countries have mostly chosen to speak Portuguese or Brazilian Portuguese, so in this chapter I will walk you through the fundamental differences and what to look for when listening to each one.

Brazilian Portuguese and Portuguese Portuguese

Vocabulary

The biggest differences lie in vocabulary, and most of them are hilarious, so be aware!

Brazil	Portugal	English
abridor de garrafas ou saca-rolhas	saca-rolhas	cork-screw
abridor de latas	abre-latas	can opener
açougue	talho	butcher shop
comissária de bordo	hospedeira de bordo	flight attendant

água-viva ou medusa	água-viva alforreca ou medusa	jelly fish
água sanitária	água sanitária, lixívia	bleach
AIDS	SIDA (Síndrome de Imuno-Deficiência Adquirida)	AIDS
alho-poró	alho-porro	leek
Amsterdã	Amsterdão	Amsterdam
aquarela	aguarela	water colours
arquivo (de computador)	ficheiro	file
aterrissagem	aterragem	landing
banheiro, toalete, toilettes, lavabo, sanitário	casa de banho, lavabos, quarto-de-banho, sanitários, w.c.	bathroom, restroom
bonde	eléctrico	tram
brócolis	brócolos	broccoli
café da manhã, desjejum, parva	pequeno almoço, desjejum	breakfast
calcinha	cuecas femininas	panties
caminhão ou camião (linguagem oral)	camião	truck
caminhonete, van, perua	carrinha	pickup truck
camiseta	camisola	t-shirt
camisola	camisa de dormir	night gown
canadense	canadiano	Canadian
câncer	cancro	cancer
caqui (fruit)	dióspiro	persimmons
carona	boleia	car ride
carro conversível	carro descapotável	convertible
carta/carteira de habilitação, carteira de motorista, carta	carta de condução	driver's license
carteira de identidade ou Registro Geral/RG	bilhete de identidade/BI/ cartão do cidadão	ID

chaveiro	porta-chaves ou chaveiro	key chain
cílio, pestana, celha	pestana	eye lashes
concreto	betão	concrete
descarga	autoclismo	flush (toilet)
decolagem	Descolagem	take-off
diretor (de cinema)	realizador	director(cinema)
dublagem	dobragem	dubbing
durex, fita adesiva	fita gomada, fita-cola, fita adesiva	scotch tape
escanteio	pontapé de canto	corner
esparadrapo, bandeide (band-aid)	penso, penso-rápido	adhesive tape
estação de trem	gare, estação	train station
estrada de ferro, ferrovia	caminho de ferro, ferrovia	railway
favela	bairro de lata	slum
fila (de pessoas)	fila ou bicha	line
fones de ouvido	auscultadores, auriculares, fones	earphones
Frankfurt	Francoforte	Frankfurt
freio, breque	travão, freio	break (car)
a gangue, a gang	o gang, o gangue	gang
gol	golo	gol
gole	golo	sip, or swallow
goleiro	guarda redes	goalie
grama, relva	relva	grass
grampeador	agrafador	stapler
guitarra	guitarra elétrica	electric guitar
Irã	Irão	Iran
Islã	Islão	Islam
isopor	esferovite	Styrofoam
israelense, israelita	israelita	Israeli

legal	fixe, giro	legal
maiô	fato-de-banho	one piece bathing suit
mamadeira	biberão	nursing bottle
metrô	metro, metropolitano	subway
Moscou	Moscovo	Moscow
Mouse	Rato	mouse
nadadeiras, pé-de-pato	barbatanas	fins (feet)
ônibus	autocarro	bus
ônibus espacial, nave espacial, espaçonave, astronave	vaivém, veículo espacial recuperável	space bus, space vehicle, spaceship
pebolim (ou totó)	matraquilhos	foosball
perua, van	carrinha	van
pinha, fruta-do-conde	anona	its a local fruit
polonês, polaco	polaco	Polish
privada sanitária, vaso sanitário ou privada	retrete ou sanita	toilet
rúgbi, rugby	râguebi, rugby	rugbi
salva-vidas ou guarda-vidas	salva-vidas ou nadador-salvador	life guard
secretária eletrônica	atendedor de chamadas	answering machine
sunga ou calção de banho	calções de banho, calção de banho	speedo
sutiã, soutien, soutien-gorge	soutien, sutiã	bra
tcheco, checo	checo	tchec
tela	ecrã	screen
telefone celular (ou simplesmente celular), aparelho de telefonia celular	telemóvel	cellphone
terno	fato	suit
time, equipe	equipa, equipe	time
tiro de meta	pontapé de baliza	goal kick

torcida	claque	fans, cheering
trem, composição ferroviária	comboio	train
Vietnã	Vietname	Vietnam
violão	guitarra	acoustic guitar
xícara	chávena	cup

Pronunciation

For Brazilians, the Portuguese pronunciation is very strange, and very funny at times, here's why. Brazilian speakers pronounce both the stressed and unstressed syllables and speak in a slower more cadenced rythm, while Portuguese speakers tend to pronounce only the stressed syllables and speak much faster:

Brazilian pronunciation	Portuguese pronunciation
menino	M'nino
gaveta	G'veta
vamos	V'mos

Conclusion

Now, Embark on Your Own Adventure!

Now you are ready to go out there and start communicating in the basic Portuguese that you have learned from this book. Keep in mind that you have not learned how to say *everything* in Portuguese, but you are equipped to make a great start and work your way around using what you now know. Don't forget the basic language skills that you have learned in this book. If you don't know how to say something, ask, use context clues, describe it using the language that you know, and you will eventually find the answer.

Don't worry about looking silly and just do your best to learn from the mistakes you make! Keep a journal to write about your experiences and the new things that you are learning every day. Though it's not always easy and sometimes rather frustrating, traveling abroad is one of the most rewarding experiences you will have. I hope this book has prepared you well and wish you many exciting and fulfilling adventures in your travels!

To your success,

Dagny Taggart
Olívia Junqueira

>> Get The Full Portuguese Online Course With Audio Lessons <<

If you truly want to learn Portuguese 300% FASTER, then hear this out.

I've partnered with the most revolutionary language teachers to bring you the very best Portuguese online course I've ever seen. It's a mind-blowing program specifically created for language hackers such as ourselves. It will allow you learn Portuguese 3x faster, straight from the comfort of your own home, office, or wherever you may be. It's like having an unfair advantage!

The Online Course consists of:

+ 185 Built-In Lessons
+ 98 Interactive Audio Lessons
+ 24/7 Support to Keep You Going

The program is extremely engaging, fun, and easy-going. You won't even notice you are learning a complex foreign language from scratch. And before you realize it, by the time you go through all the lessons you will officially become a truly solid Portuguese speaker.

Old classrooms are a thing of the past. It's time for a language revolution.

If you'd like to go the extra mile, follow the link below and let the revolution begin

>> http://www.bitly.com/Portuguese-Course <<

CHECK OUT THE COURSE »

PS: Can I Ask You a Quick Favor?

If you liked the book please leave a nice review on Amazon! I'd absolutely love to hear your feedback. Please go to Amazon right now (following the link below), and write down a quick line sharing with me your experience. I personally read ALL the reviews there, and I'm thrilled to hear your feedback and honest motivation. It's what keeps me going, and helps me improve everyday =)

Please go Amazon now and drop a quick review sharing your experience!

***

Thanks a lot!

***

**ONCE YOU'RE BACK,
FLIP THE PAGE!
BONUS CHAPTER AHEAD
=)**

Preview Of "Learn Spanish In 7 DAYS! - The Ultimate Crash Course To Learn The Basics of the Spanish Language In No Time"

Are You ready? It's Time To Learn Spanish!

Most people are daunted by the idea of learning a language. They think it's impossible, even unfathomable. I remember as a junior in high school, watching footage of Jackie O giving a speech in French. I was so impressed and inspired by the ease at which she spoke this other language of which I could not understand one single word.

At that moment, I knew I had to learn at least one foreign language. I started with Spanish, later took on Mandarin, and most recently have started learning Portuguese. No matter how challenging and unattainable it may seem, millions of people have done it. You do NOT have to be a genius to learn another language. You DO have to be willing to take risks and make mistakes, sometimes even make a fool of yourself, be dedicated, and of course, practice, practice, practice!

This book will only provide you with the basics in order to get started learning the Spanish language. It is geared towards those who are planning to travel to a Spanish-speaking country and covers many common scenarios you may find yourself in so feel free to skip around to the topic that is most prudent to you at the moment. It is also focused on the Spanish of Latin America rather than Spain. Keep in mind, every Spanish-speaking country has some language details specific to them so it would be essential to do some research on the specific country or countries that you will visit.

I will now list some tips that I have found useful and should be very helpful to you in your journey of learning Spanish. I don't wish you luck because that will not get you anywhere- reading this book, dedicating yourself, and taking some risks will!

Important note

Due to the nature of this book (it contains charts, graphs, and so on), you will better your reading experience by setting your device on *LANDSCAPE* mode! (In case you're using an electronic device like Kindle).

Language Tips

Tip #1 - Keep an Open Mind

It may seem obvious but you must understand that languages are very different from each other. You cannot expect them to translate word for word. *'There is a black dog'* will not translate word for word with the same word order in Spanish. You have to get used to the idea of translating WHOLE ideas. So don't find yourself saying, *"Why is everything backwards in Spanish?"* because it may seem that way many times. Keep your mind open to the many differences that you will find in the language that go far beyond just the words.

Tip #2 - Take Risks

Be fearless. Talk to as many people as you can. The more practice you get the better and don't worry about looking like a fool when you say, *"I am pregnant"* rather than *"I am embarrassed,"* which as you will find out can be a common mistake. If anyone is laughing remember they are not laughing at you. Just laugh with them, move on, and LEARN from it, which brings us to our next tip.

Tip #3 - Learn from your Mistakes

It doesn't help to get down because you made one more mistake when trying to order at a restaurant, take a taxi, or just in a friendly conversation. Making mistakes is a HUGE part of learning a language. You have to put yourself out there as we said and be willing to make tons of mistakes! Why? Because what can you do with mistakes. You can LEARN from them. If you never make a mistake, you probably are not learning as much as you could. So every time you mess up when trying to communicate, learn from it, move on, and keep your head up!

Tip #4 - Immerse yourself in the language

If you're not yet able to go to a Spanish-speaking country, try to pretend that you are. Surround yourself with Spanish. Listen to music in Spanish, watch movies, TV shows, in Spanish. Play games on your phone, computer, etc. in Spanish. Another great idea is to actually put your phone, computer, tablet and/or other electronic devices in Spanish. It can be frustrating at first but in the end this exposure will definitely pay off.

Tip #5 - Start Thinking in Spanish

I remember being a senior in high school and working as a lifeguard at a fairly deserted pool. While I was sitting and staring at the empty waters, I would speak to myself or think to myself (to not seem so crazy) in Spanish. I would describe my surroundings, talk about what I had done and what I was going to do, etc. While I was riding my bike, I would do the same thing. During any activity when you don't need to talk or think about anything else, keep your brain constantly going in Spanish to get even more practice in the language. So get ready to turn off the English and jumpstart your Spanish brain!

Tip #6 - Label your Surroundings/Use Flashcards

When I started to learn Portuguese, I bought an excellent book that included stickers so that you could label your surroundings. So I had stickers all over my parents' house from the kitchen to the bathroom that labeled the door, the dishes, furniture, parts of the house, etc. It was a great, constant reminder of how to say these objects in another language. You can just make your own labels and stick them all over the house and hope it doesn't bother your family or housemates too much!

Tip #7 - Use Context clues, visuals, gestures, expressions, etc.

If you don't understand a word that you have heard or read, look or listen to the surrounding words and the situation to help you. If you are in a restaurant and your friend says, "I am going to ??? a sandwich." You can take a guess that she said *order* or *eat* but you don't have to understand every word in order to understand the general meaning. When you are in a conversation use gestures, expressions, and things around you to help communicate your meaning. Teaching English as a second language to young learners taught me this. If you act everything out, you are more likely to get your point across. If you need to say the word *bird* and you don't know how you can start flapping your arms and chirping and then you will get your point across and possibly learn how to say *bird*. It may seem ridiculous but as I said, you have to be willing to look silly to learn another language and this greatly helps your language communication and learning.

Tip #8 - Circumlocution

Circumlo... what? This is just a fancy word for describing something when you don't know how to say it. If you are looking to buy an umbrella and don't know how to say it, what can you do? You can describe it using words you know. You can say, it is something used for the rain that opens and closes and then hopefully someone will understand you, help you, and maybe teach you how to say this word. Using circumlocution is excellent language practice and is much better than just giving up when you don't know how to say a word. So keep talking even if you have a limited vocabulary. Say what you can and describe or act out what you can't!

SECTION 1: THE BASICS

Chapter 1: Getting the Pronunciation Down

Below I will break down general Spanish pronunciation for the whole alphabet dividing it into vowels and consonants. One great thing about Spanish is that the letters almost always stay consistent as far as what sound they make. Unlike English in which the vowels can make up to 27 different sounds depending on how they are mixed. Be thankful that you don't have to learn English or at least have already learned English. There are of course some sounds in Spanish that we never make in English and you possibly have never made in your life. So get ready to start moving your mouth and tongue in a new way that may seem strange at first but as I keep saying, practice makes perfect!

The charts on the next page will explain how to say the letter, pronounce it, and if there is an example in an English word of how to say it I put it in the right column.

Vowel Sounds

Vowel	How to say the letter	How to pronounce it in a word	As in...
a	Ah	Ah	T<u>a</u>co
e	Eh	Eh	<u>E</u>gg
i	Ee	Ee	<u>Ea</u>sy
o	Oh	Oh	<u>O</u>pen
u	Oo	Oo	B<u>oo</u>k

Consonant Sounds

Consonant	How to say the letter	How to pronounce it in a word	As in...
b	beh	similar to English b	
c	ceh	k after *a, o,* or *u* s after *e* or *i*	cat cereal
ch	cheh	ch	cheese
d	deh	a soft d (place your tongue at the back of your upper teeth)	three
f	efe	F	free
g	geh	h before i or e g before a, o, u	him go
h	ache	silent	
j	hota	H	him
k	kah	K	karaoke
l	ele	like English l with tongue raised to roof of mouth	
ll	eye	Y	yes
m	eme	M	money
n	ene	N	no
ñ	enye	Ny	canyon
p	peh	like English p but you don't aspirate	

Consonants continued

Consonant	How to say the letter	How to pronounce it in a word	As in...
Q	koo	k (q is always followed by u like English)	quilt
R	ere	* at the beginning of a word you must roll your r's by vibrating tongue at roof of mouth * in the middle of	

			a word it sounds like a soft d	
rr	erre	roll your r's as mentioned above	
S	ese	Like English s	sorry
T	teh	a soft English t, the tongue touches the back of the upper teeth	
V	veh	like Spanish b	boots

Consonants continued

Consonant	How to say the letter	How to pronounce it in a word	As in…
w	dobleveh	like English w	water
x	equis	*Between vowels and at the end of a word, it sounds like the English *ks*. *At the beginning of a word, it sounds like the letter *s*.	*box *sorry
y	igriega	like English y	yellow
z	seta	s	six

Note: If you're not sure how to pronounce a word, one thing you can do is type it in *Google translate* then click on the little speaker icon in the bottom left corner to hear the correct pronunciation.

To check out the rest of "Learn Spanish In 7 DAYS! - The Ultimate Crash Course To Learning The Basics of The Spanish Language In No Time", ***go to Amazon and look for it right now!***

Check Out My Other Books

Are you ready to exceed your limits? Then pick a book from the one below and start learning yet another new language. I can't imagine anything more fun, fulfilling, and exciting!

If you'd like to see the entire list of language guides (there are a ton more!), go to:

>>http://www.amazon.com/Dagny-Taggart/e/B00K54K6CS/<<

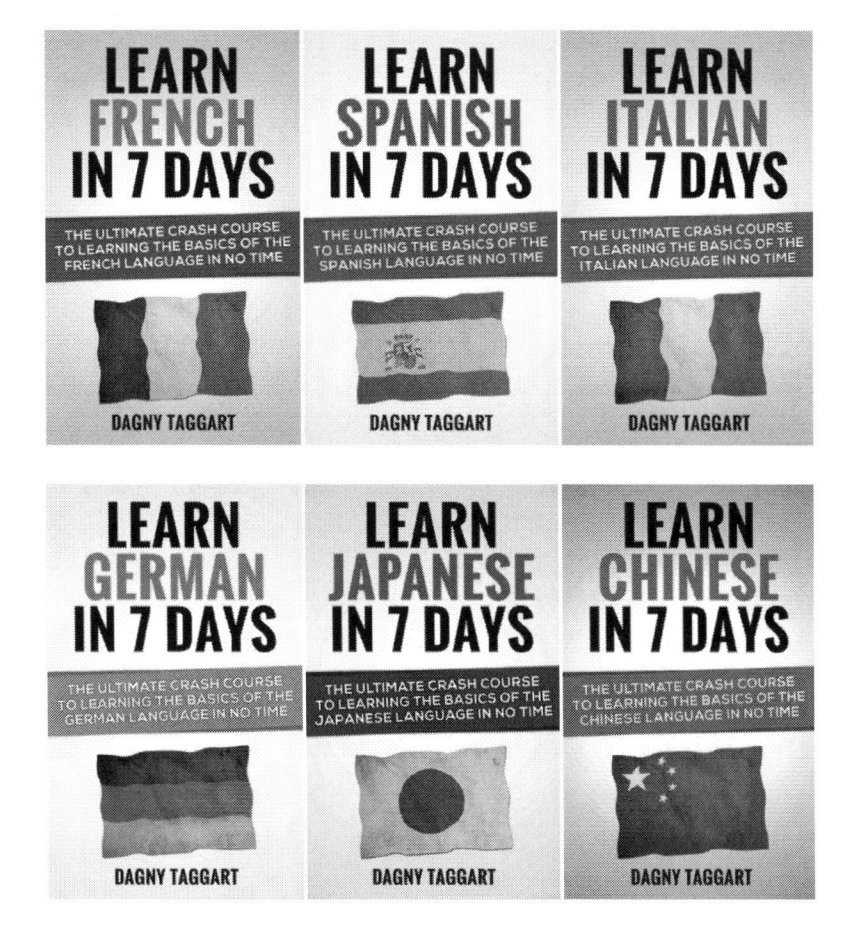

About the Author

Dagny Taggart is a language enthusiast and polyglot who travels the world, inevitably picking up more and more languages along the way.

Taggart's true passion became learning languages after she realized the incredible connections with people that it fostered. Now she just can't get enough of it. Although it's taken time, she has acquired vast knowledge on the best and fastest ways to learn languages. But the truth is, she is driven simply by her motive to build exceptional links and bonds with others.

She is inspired everyday by the individuals she meets across the globe. For her, there's simply not anything as rewarding as practicing languages with others because she gets to make friends with people from all that come from a variety of cultures. This, in turn, has broadened her mind and thinking more than she would have ever imagined it could.

Of course, as a result of her constant travels, Taggart has become an expert on planning trips and making the most of time spent out of what she calls her "base" town. She jokes that she's practically at the nomad status now, but she's more content to live that way.

She knows how to live on a manageable budget weather she's in Paris or Phnom Penh. She knows how to seek out the adventures and thrills, no doubt, lying in wait at any city she visits. She knows that reflection on each every experience is significant if she wants to grow as a traveler and student of the world's cultures.

Because of this, Taggart chooses to share her understanding of languages and travel so that others, too, can experience the same life-altering benefits she has.

Printed in Great Britain
by Amazon.co.uk, Ltd.,
Marston Gate.